THE FIRST-TIME HOMEOWNER'S SURVIVAL GUIDE

THE FIRST-TIME HOMEOWNER'S SURVIVAL GUIDE

A Crash Course in Dealing with Repairs,
Renovations, Property Tax Issues,
and Other Potential Disasters

SID DAVIS

American Management Association

New York • Atlanta • Brussels • Chicago • Mexico City • San Francisco
Shanghai • Tokyo • Toronto • Washington, D.C.

Special discounts on bulk quantities of AMACOM books are available to corporations, professional associations, and other organizations. For details, contact Special Sales Department, AMACOM, a division of American Management Association, 1601 Broadway, New York, NY 10019. Tel: 212-903-8316. Fax: 212-903-8083. E-mail: specialsls@amanet.org Website: www.amacombooks.org/go/specialsales To view all AMACOM titles go to: www.amacombooks.org

This publication is designed to provide accurate and authoritative information in regard to the subject matter covered. It is sold with the understanding that the publisher is not engaged in rendering legal, accounting, or other professional service. If legal advice or other expert assistance is required, the services of a competent professional person should be sought.

REALTOR® is a registered collective membership mark that identifies a real estate professional who is a member of the National Association of REALTORS® and subscribes to its strict Code of Ethics. AMACOM uses these names throughout this book in initial capital letters or ALL CAPITAL letters for editorial purposes only, with no intention of trademark violation.

Library of Congress Cataloging-in-Publication Data

Davis, Sid.
    The first-time homeowner's survival guide : a crash course in dealing with repairs, renovations, property tax issues, and other potential disasters / Sid Davis.
        p.   cm.
    Includes bibliographical references and index.
    ISBN-13: 978-0-8144-7372-6
    ISBN-10: 0-8144-7372-5
    1. Home ownership—United States.   I. Title.

HD7287.82.U6D38   2007
643—dc22   2007003725

Printing number

10   9   8   7   6   5   4   3   2   1

CONTENTS

A comprehensive glossary along with printable checklists and worksheets are available at www.sid-davis.com by clicking on the book banner.

PREFACE

Your home is likely to be the biggest investment you'll ever make. You need to care for it and nurture it, not only because it's where you live, but because your financial future and emotional well-being may well depend on it. It's therefore critical to keep it in good condition. That way it will be a joy to live in and also give you maximum return when you sell. How to do this is the goal of this book.

If you're a first-time homeowner who has just moved in and feels overwhelmed, or you want to brush up on the nuts and bolts of making the most of your home, this book is for you. Some of the important items contained in the following chapters are:

- Easy-to-follow explanations and charts that illustrate how different systems and components work to make your home a marvel of comfort and convenience.
- Tips and how-to instructions for handling easy repairs on your own, even if you're not sure how a screwdriver works.
- Suggestions for hiring and working with handymen and contractors on those projects for which you need professional help, along with tips on how not to get ripped off.
- Tips on which upgrades add to the value of your home and which ones don't.
- Checklists at the end of each chapter to remind you of things to do to keep your home's components working smoothly. These checklists

will also keep you on top of what needs to be done to make sure your home weathers the seasonal changes.

- How to avoid losing thousands of dollars in unneeded repairs and scams that target homeowners.
- Money-saving tips on buying insurance, replacing appliances, choosing floor coverings and other materials, and making upgrades.

In other words, this is a book you'll want to keep in a handy place so you can refer to it often when pesky homeowner problems come at you fast, demanding prompt action and/or a credit card number.

Also, for a comprehensive glossary along with printable checklists and worksheets, go to www.sid-davis.com, and click on the book banner.

THE FIRST-TIME HOMEOWNER'S SURVIVAL GUIDE

CHAPTER 1

YOUR HOME'S ELECTRICAL SYSTEM 101

In this chapter you'll learn:

- ✓ How your home's electrical system works
- ✓ Potential electrical problems to look out for
- ✓ Quick and easy electrical fixes you can handle on your own
- ✓ When you should call an electrician and how to hire one
- ✓ A troubleshooting guide that will help you track down and solve problems

Few things are more feared, less understood, and more discouraging to a new homeowner than the electrical system. Fortunately, it doesn't have to be that way. If you can chew gum and tie your running-shoe laces at the same time, you can understand and perform common electrical maintenance. It's that straightforward! Even when you're hiring professionals you need to have a basic understanding of your electrical system, if for no other reason than to understand what you're being charged.

HOW TO READ THE POWER METER AND MAKE SURE YOU'RE NOT OVERCHARGED

One question many homeowners ask about their electrical service is how they can be sure the power company is not overcharging them. Meter readers are in a hurry and can misread the meter. Sometimes that can be in your favor, other times the bill goes up dramatically and you wonder why. You can solve the uncertainty be reading the electric meter dials yourself and keeping a log of your usage.

The power company charges you for power used in blocks of 1,000 watts used for one hour, or one kilowatt-hour (kwh). If you look closely at your electric meter, you'll notice a small spinning wheel in the middle. When there's current flowing, the small wheel is spinning, which means it's costing you.

There are two types of meters for recording electrical usage. One is a meter similar to the odometer on your car, where you can read the kilowatts used just as you would read the miles driven. The other meter has five dials numbered like a clock face, except that the numbers run from 0 to 9 counter-clock wise (see Figure 1-1).

To read the dials, simply start with the left-hand dial and jot down the numbers. If the pointer lies between two numbers, always use the lower number even if the hand is almost on a higher number. For example, in Figure 1-1 the meter reading would be 06573.

If you want to verify the power company's reading, read the meter the same day the meter reader stops by, and again the following month. Then compare the usage to what's shown on your power bill.

Figure 1-1.

For example, the typical power bill in Figure 1-2 shows the previous and current meter readings, 5142 and 6075. Subtracting the two readings shows that 933 kilowatts were used this billing period. If your meter reading varies more than a few kwh from what the billing shows, call your power company's customer service number on your statement.

Some utilities charge more per kilowatt-hour over a certain amount, and/ or for usage during peak hours (1 P.M. to 8 P.M., for instance).

In Figure 1-2 for example, the first 400 kilowatts cost just over 6.9 cents per kwh. The next 533 kilowatts cost over 7.8 cents per kwh, for a total of $69.70 for the billing period.

Of course, power costs vary depending on the area you live in, but check your bill for the power company's website. They usually have special rates and programs that can help you lower your power costs.

Figure 1-2.

METER NUMBER	SERVICE PERIOD From To	ELAPSED DAYS	METER READINGS Previous Current	METER MULTIPLIER	AMOUNT USED THIS MONTH
39066428	Jul 28, 2006 Aug 25, 2006	28	5142 6075	1.0	933 kwh

NEW CHARGES - 08/06	UNITS	COST PER UNIT	CHARGE
Basic Charge - 1P			0.98
Energy Charge 1st Block	400 kwh	0.0693600	27.74
Energy Charge 2nd Block	533 kwh	0.0787200	41.96

THE DANGER OF WORKING WITH ELECTRICAL POWER

Broadly speaking, the electricity that powers your MP3 player, computer, or refrigerator is the same as lightning; the only difference is that one is controlled and the other is raw, untapped electrical energy.

When the power company generates electrical energy and distributes it over a long distances, it needs to maintain a high voltage in the lines. It's helpful to compare voltage to water pressure. A lot of pressure (lbs. per square inch) is needed to push water through the pipes to the those homes on the system that are farthest removed. Likewise, lots of electrical pressure (*volts*) is needed to get power out to the power company's farthest removed customers.

Another important electrical measurement is *amps*, which is the amount of electrical power you have to work with. Using the water analogy, the amount of water in a system is measured in gallons, whereas the amount of power coming into your home is measured in amps. For example, to show the difference between volts and amps, shuffling your feet across the carpet may generate a charge of about 400 volts. That this charge will jump from you to another object shows there's a lot of pressure. But it's not dangerous because there are so few amps involved, just a lot of voltage.

But if you were to up the amps to the 15 or so that you find in a 120 volt household circuit, it's a different story—now it's enough to kill you if you get careless.

The good news is that electricity follows natural laws and is highly predictable. The downside is if you don't follow the rules there can be unpleasant consequences.

So it's important to keep in mind the following safety rules as you work on your home's electrical system.

IT ALL STARTS WITH THE SERVICE PANEL

Safety starts with knowing where the service panel (sometimes called "breaker box") or fuse box (if you have an older system) is located. This is where you can cut off power to different parts of the house. If you see a smoking or sparking receptacle box, the service panel is where you need to run to and cut off the power. Details on how this works is covered in the next section.

The panel is usually located in the basement, a closet, near the back door, or even outside near the electric meter. So your first step is to locate your service panel or fuse box and open it up. You'll notice a row or double row of on/off switches or round fuses. Each on/off switch (fuse) in the box has a wire or circuit going from it to somewhere in your house, whether it's could your living room wall receptacles or your refrigerator. If you were to flip that switch to off, that particular circuit would be dead, and it would be safe to work on.

Working Safely

With that introduction, the following tips will help you work with your electrical system safely:

•   Always shut off the power to the circuit you plan on working with. If you're not sure which breaker (or fuse) goes to that circuit, plug in a light and start flipping breaker switches until the light goes out. It doesn't hurt to tape the "off" breaker (or remove the fuse) to prevent it from accidentally being turned on while you're working on the circuit. One home renovator—who shall remain nameless—was working on some wiring when a helper flipped all the breakers on. Luckily the owner wasn't hurt, but the short destroyed the electric meter and the owner got a don't-you-know-what-you're-doing lecture from the power company rep.

• Make sure all of the breakers are correctly labeled. (How to label the circuits in the breaker box is explained later in the Mapping Your Electrical System section.)

• Use a circuit tester to make sure wires are not hot (meaning there's no electricity flowing through them). You can find inexpensive circuit testers in any hardware store. A tester is simply two probes (wires) connected to a light or buzzer (see Figure 1-3). When the wire is hot, the light will glow or the buzzer will sound.

• Never stand on a wet or damp floor when working with electricity. Use dry boards or a rubber mat.

Figure 1-3.

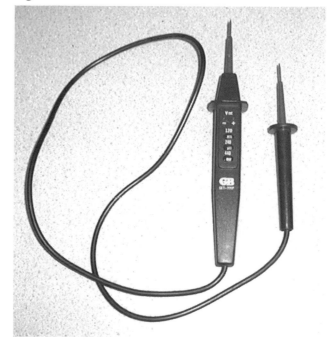

• Avoid touching plumbing, fixtures, radiators, or metal ducts while working with electricity. If you accidentally touch a live wire and a metal pipe, you could get seriously hurt.

• Never touch the wires going into your service panel. They are still live even if you have pulled the main disconnect or flipped all the breakers off.

• If you have overhead wires, be careful moving aluminum ladders around them. Aluminum is a great electrical conductor, and touching an overhead wire with the ladder can give you a bad shock.

• Use tools with rubber or plastic covered handles.

THE SERVICE PANEL: HOW IT WORKS

Power from the utility company goes from their pole or underground line to the electric meter and from there to the service panel or fuse box (see Figure 1-4).

Figure 1-4.

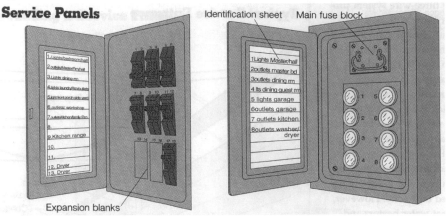

Service Panels

Identification sheet   Main fuse block

Expansion blanks

If your power comes from an overhead line, you'll see a grey cylinder or transformer mounted on the pole. If the power comes from underground wires, there'll be a large metal box somewhere on your property that contains the transformer.

The transformer's job is to reduce the main line's voltage down to what your house can handle. Three wires go from the transformer to your service entrance and meter then to your service panel or breaker box. From there, wires or circuits run throughout your house to the switches and outlets.

The first thing you want to become familiar with is the location of the main disconnect, which cuts all power to your house. Some breaker boxes have a main switch at the top of the panel; others don't and you have to look outside to where the meter is, as in Figure 1-5.

If you have a fuse box, the main disconnect is likely a double fuse block with a handle you pull out to cut the power, as illustrated on the right in Figure 1-4.

Both the breakers and the fuses have the same job, which is to protect the electrical system. For example, if lightning were to strike close by and overload the system it would flip the breaker off or cause the metal connector in the fuse to melt. To restore power you just push the breaker back to the "on" position. But if you have a fuse-protected system, you would need to replace the fuse. It's always a good idea to keep several spare fuses where they're easy to find, since having no fuses on hand means no video games and melted ice cream.

Some other conditions that can trip a breaker or blow a fuse are:

• Putting too many items on a circuit.
• Overloading a circuit with an appliance that pulls more power than the circuit is designed for. Common examples are hair dryers, heaters,

Figure 1-5.

and frying pans. Shorts from frayed electric cords can also trip a breaker.

- A spike in the power company's power grid. (This is why you need a surge protector for your electronics.)
- An electric motor or appliance malfunctions, water getting into in a receptacle or switch, or a loose wire touching a metal object.

HELPFUL ELECTRICAL HOW-TO WEBSITES

www.selfhelpandmore.com/switchoutlet/index.htm
www.electrical-online.com/Replacingabreakerinyourpanel.htm
www.doityourself.com/stry/typesfusescircuits

Mapping Your Circuits

Once you know how to cut off the main power, the next step to becoming buddies with your electrical system is knowing what circuits control which receptacles and switches. If the electrician who wired the home or the previous owner labeled the circuits similar to those in Figure 1-4, you're ahead of the game. But if it's unlabeled, you'll need to take the time to map the system and label each circuit.

A *word of caution*: If you're a new homeowner or haven't paid too much attention to your electrical system, you should verify that the labels on the breakers or fuses are accurate. With older homes especially, previous owners may have changed wiring around and not noted it on the panel.

Five reasons why it's important to map your system are:

1. When you replace a receptacle or switch, cutting power to only that circuit rather than the whole house saves you the frustration of resetting all the clocks, and avoids having to turn off the electronics and interrupt others using power in the house.

2. If a circuit becomes overloaded and flips a breaker, you can narrow down the problem fast.

3. You can keep track of what items you put on a circuit so you don't exceed it's capacity. For example, if you turn on a hair dryer and a breaker flips, you'll know at once which circuit has too much of a load.

4. If you need to add outlets, you can tell whether the nearest circuit can handle an increased load safely.

5. By knowing the total capacity (amps) of your system and what you're using, you can calculate whether you can add additional circuits. For example, say you want to put in a new patio and add power for lights and a sound system, will your present system handle it?

Before you start mapping your system, you should know how many amps you have to work with, or your system's electrical capacity.

DETERMINING YOUR ELECTRICAL SYSTEM'S CAPACITY

As mentioned above, the starting point for all electrical maintenance and improvement projects is the fuse box or the circuit breaker panel. When there's trouble on a circuit, such as a short or overload, the breakers or fuses save the day by shutting off the current.

Some older homes, however, can have a smaller, separate fuse box or breaker box added to the main electrical system to protect it when they're adding a high load appliance, such as central air-conditioning. This satellite box doesn't add to the total amps available, but adds a layer of protection.

Opening the panel, you'll notice that there are three wires coming into your fuse or breaker box from the meter: a black, a red, and a white wire. The red and black wires carry 120 volts, and the white is neutral.

Smaller circuits that power lights, receptacles, and small appliances will use the black and white wires. The white or neutral wires for all the circuits are connected to a metal strip, called the neutral busbar. The black or hot wires are connected to the fuse or breaker to power that circuit. For example, if you were to add a new 15-amp circuit, you would run a plastic sheathed 3-wire cable from where you want the power back to the panel. The white wire and bare copper ground wire would connect to the neutral busbar while the black wire would connect to the fuse or breaker.

For most circuits the black and white wires furnish about 15 to 20 amps at 120 volts. However, high load appliances, such a dryers, range/ovens, air conditioners, or shop welders require more voltage. These appliances require both the 120 volt black and red wires (totaling 240 volts) and may draw up to 50 amps.

Here's the really important part:

Your electrical panel can handle only so many amps.

Older homes that haven't been upgraded in sixty years probably have only a small 30-amp to 60-amp fuse box. That's a real underachiever system by today's standards. Some later systems have 90-amp services, which you may still find in older homes that haven't been upgraded. Although 100-amp services are still common in many homes, with today's power-hungry appliances and electronics, 150 to 200 amps are better.

However, if your home has a gas range/oven, a gas water heater, and a gas clothes dryer, you could get along nicely with 90 amps or less.

Somewhere in your panel or main disconnect will be the number of amps your service is rated for. For example, in Figure 1-5, the amp rating—150—is molded onto the end of the breaker switch.

Once you know how many amps are available, the next step is mapping your system to find out how many amps you're now using and how they're allocated among the different circuits.

HOW TO MAP YOUR ELECTRICAL SYSTEM

Two people are needed to do a thorough job. One person works at the main service panel flipping breakers or removing fuses, while the other tests outlets, appliances, and switches with a circuit tester, similar to the one shown in Figure 1-3. The following five easy steps show how:

1. *Sketch the floor plan.* Draw a floor plan of each room and mark all the receptacles, switches, and light fixtures. Sketch in appliances that are connected directly to the panel, such as electric ranges, water heaters, dryers, and air conditioners.

2. *Number the circuits.* At the main service panel, number each circuit breaker or fuse with stick-on labels. Some panels may already be numbered as in Figure 1-4.

3. Set up the test. Work on one room at a time. Turn on all the lights, lamps, and appliances in the room. If the room has double receptacles, plug a light into each. Don't turn on appliances that have their own circuit.

4. *Record what's on the circuit.* The person at the service panel turns off the first breaker or fuse. On the floor plan the helper writes down the number of the circuit or fuse and which fixtures, switches, and receptacles are affected. For example, on circuit #1 you list everything that went out, for example, the ceiling light, hall light, and three of the five receptacles in the living room.

One homeowner plugged her hair dryer into the receptacles rather than using a circuit tester to see which ones were hot; another one used a small lamp. Both worked great in identifying what was working.

5. *Repeat the process for the other circuits.* Flip circuit #1 back on and repeat the process for all the breakers or fuses in the panel. When you're through, each circuit should have a label stuck next to it detailing what it controls. Do the same for any 240-volt double breakers or fuses that control the range, dryer, water heater, or air conditioner.

Now that you've mapped your electrical system and understand it, if a fuse blows or breaker trips from a short or overload, it won't be panic time. You'll be able to go right to the affected circuit and troubleshoot. However, there's a big red warning flag waving here if this happens often. Blown fuses mean your electrical system may have problems and is not meeting your needs. It could be time to think about upgrading.

DOES YOUR SYSTEM HAVE THE CAPACITY IT SHOULD?

As mentioned above: *Amps* are how much current a conductor can carry, and *volts* are electrical pressure. The third important measurement, *watts,* tells you:

- How much load or what appliances you can put on a circuit.
- How many watts, or 1,000-watt bundles called kilowatts, the power company uses to bill you for electricity used.
- How efficient your appliances are by comparing how many watts they use. This is disclosed on tags or labels on all electrical appliances.

To calculate the wattage a circuit can handle, multiply amps times the volts. (In the United States, voltage is standardized at 120 and 240.) For example, a standard 15-amp circuit times 120 volts equals 1,800 watts.

Most kitchen circuits are 20 amps, so multiplying by 120 volts equals 2,400 watts—enough to allow you to run the coffee maker and toaster at the same time.

If your kitchen circuit is only a 15-amp circuit, however, you know that the total appliances you can use at the same time can't consume more than 1,800 watts. For example, if you're using a hair dryer on turbo setting that uses 1000 watts, while at the same time warming up an iron that consumes another 1000 watts, and both on the same circuit, you're going to burn out a fuse or flip a breaker. The simple math is: 1000 + 1000 = 2000 watts on a 1,800 watt circuit.

Table 1-1 gives you an idea of some common appliance wattage ratings.

Ideally, the wattage of any one appliance should not be more than 80

Table 1-1. Typical wattage ratings.

Appliance	Rating	Appliance	Rating
Window air conditioner	800–1500	Garbage disposal unit	500–1000
Electric blanket	150–500	Hair dryer	100–1400
Blender	200–400	Hot plate	600–1000
Toaster oven	1400–1500	Water heater (240 amp)	2500–5000
Coffee maker	600–750	Microwave oven	650
Crock pot (2 quart)	100	Range (each burner)	5000
Dishwasher	1100	Oven	4500
Mixer	150–250	Refrigerator	150–300
Fryer (deep fat)	1200–1600	Stereo	250–500
Frying pan	1000–1200	Vacuum cleaner	300–600
Gas furnace	600–1200	Waffle iron	700–1100
Toaster	250–1000	Washing Machine	600–900

percent of a circuit's total capacity. As you can see from the figures in Table 1-1, when you have too few circuits, overloading them with extensions and appliances will cause problems.

UPGRADING YOUR ELECTRICAL SYSTEM

You should seriously consider upgrading your service if:

- The electrical system has two-wire service. Outlets take two prong plugs only and the fuse box has no bare copper ground wire. It's likely this system dates earlier than the 1940s and is a prime candidate for trouble unless you upgrade.
- You have too few outlets. Wall receptacles should be no more than 12 feet apart.
- Receptacles are not located where you need them and you have to run extension cords.
- Not all bathroom and outdoor receptacles are protected by ground-fault circuit interrupters (GFI).
- You have to unplug some appliances to run others.
- Using a high-amp appliance, such as a hairdryer, toaster, or waffle iron, flips a breaker.
- You want to add more receptacles or another circuit but there's no room in the panel.
- Your system is protected by fuses rather than circuit breakers.
- The system's amp rating is less than 100 amps. (When you're tripping breakers, it may be a good investment to go 150 or 200 amps.)
- Some of the wiring shows its sheathing is old and deteriorating from age, rodents, or environmental damage.
- You have aluminum wiring mixed with copper-wire additions.

The cost of upgrading your electrical system typically runs from $2,500 to $12,000, depending on how extensive the remodeling job is. A beginning point to determining what it will cost for your home is talk to several electrical contractors. (Tips on finding one are covered later on in the chapter.)

In most areas, upgrading the electrical system will increase your home's value equal to or more than your cost. This is an important upgrade for buyers. A new *electrical service entrance* (where the power company's lines enter your home) and a 150- or 200-amp breaker box with room for expansion are great selling points.

To determine exactly how much you will recoup, talk to a couple of appraisers who work in your area. Or have a Realtor pull up on their MLS (Multiple Listing Service) database sales of homes with upgraded electrical systems, compared with sales of homes with older systems. This should give you a good idea of what your rate-of-return will be.

It's also important to note that if you have a house fire, the insurance company usually pays to restore your home to what it was, not according to the current code. That means if your home's electrical system is not updated, you'll get a paltry check for what it would take to restore it. But the real kicker lies with the city building codes. You won't be able to rebuild your home unless you bring the electrical (and usually everything else) up to code. It can be a case of pay me now or pay me later.

While you're thinking about it, it's a good idea to contact your homeowner's insurance agent and see how your policy handles this.

WHAT ELECTRICAL REPAIRS YOU CAN DO AND WHEN TO CALL A PROFESSIONAL

Even though your electrical system may be straightforward and you don't need a physics degree to handle repairs, lack of experience or lack of the right tools means you'll occasionally need professional help. Still there are a number of problems you can handle yourself and save a few bucks, such as replacing switches, outlets, blown fuses, and worn-out breakers.

Replacing Switches

Because switches take a lot of abuse, it's amazing they last as long as they do. But when they go out, replacing them isn't difficult.

Basically, a single pole switch has two terminals. The hot wire (black) is hooked to one terminal screw and the outgoing wire (again black) is hooked to the other one. The white wire remains uninterrupted or is connected by a wire nut.

You can tell when a switch goes bad if you flip the toggle and there's a pop, flash, or burned plastic smell, and the switch no longer works.

Replacing a malfunctioning switch is easier than learning how to double-click the left mouse button. Here's how:

1. Turn off either the main power disconnect or the circuit you're working on.

2. Remove the face plate. You may have to run a razor blade along the edge to free the plate from a painted wall.

3. Remove the two screws that hold the switch to the box and pull the switch out from the box far enough to work on the connectors.

4. Notice how the black and white wires are connected to the switch. Draw a diagram so you can repeat the connections when you hook up the new switch.

5. Disconnect the wires from the switch. The wires will be connected one of two ways: either by pushing the wire into a spring loaded clip in the back, or the wire will be bent around a screw terminal and tightened (see Figure 1-6).

6. If the wire is attached with a spring clip, simply insert a screw driver tip as illustrated in Figure 1-7 and release the clip. Take the old switch to an electrical supplier or hardware store and get a similar switch.

7. Connect the wires to the switch and replace the retaining screws. Note that many switches have both screw terminals and spring clips to attach wires. If you go the screw terminal route make sure the wire loop tightens as you turn the screwdriver clockwise as in Figure 1-6.

8. If you use the spring clip to attach the wires, simply remove about a half-inch of insulation and insert the wire end into the hole in the back of the switch as in Figure 1-7.

9. Replace the mounting screws and the face place, turn on the breaker and give it a test. It should work!

Throughout the house are more complicated switches, such as two- and three-way switches, and you can replace those too. Simply follow the previously outlined steps and draw a detailed diagram of where the black and white wires go. Then take the bad switch to a supply house, match it, and hook up the wires the same way you disconnected them.

Replacing Outlets

When outlets malfunction it can be more dramatic than when a switch goes. For example, you can plug or unplug an appliance and get a bright flash, the smell of burning insulation, or a shower of sparks and a tripped breaker.

Replacing an outlet is similar to replacing a switch. Disconnect the main breaker or fuse and remove the face plate. You'll notice there can be a lot more wires. That's because outlets are sometimes wired in a series, or wires run from one outlet to several others.

Again, as you did with the switch wiring, draw a diagram of where the black and white wires go. Take the broken outlet to a electrical supply store and match it, making sure you get the right amp rating, 15 or 20. While you're at it, buy some extra outlets, because they don't always malfunction during business hours.

Replace the screws and test it. It should work.

Figure 1-6.

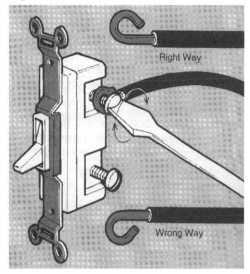

Blown Fuses

Figure 1-7.

Blown fuses can be a symptom of a worn out switch or outlet, or a short. The first two are easy to replace, but a short may be more difficult to track down. But under no circumstances replace a fuse with one that has a higher amp rating than the circuit is rated for, not even long enough to finish your favorite TV program.

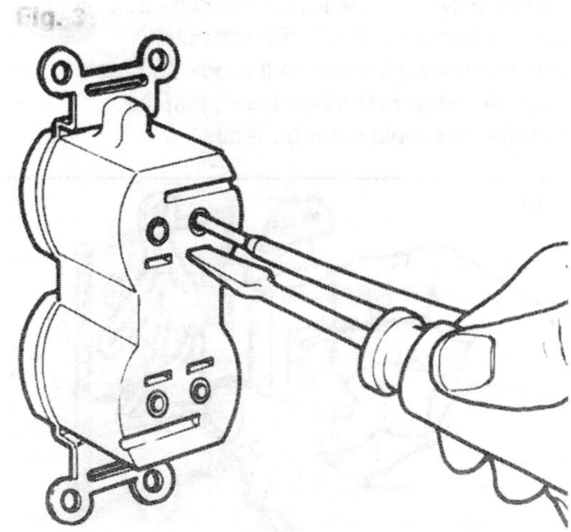

For example, replacing 15-amp fuses with 20-amp fuses to keep them from blowing is asking for trouble. *Overfusing*, as it's often called, is a major contributor to over 40,000 electrically caused fires and 350 deaths a year, according to the U.S. Consumer Product Safety Commission.

If you replace a fuse and it burns out again, follow these steps:

- Determine what's on the dead circuit. Here's where your circuit map comes in handy. You may have overloaded the circuit in an unthinking moment by plugging in a high wattage item or an extension cord into the nearest outlet.

• Check the switches and outlets for scorch marks or melted connectors.

• If you have appliances on the circuit, plug them into another circuit and see if one of them has shorted out and is causing your fuse to blow. If this is the culprit, replace the appliance.

• If possible, check the wiring from the box to the outlets. A rodent may have chewed the insulation and caused a short.

If after trying these suggestions the circuit still blows fuses, it's time to call an electrician and hunt for your checkbook.

Malfunctioning Breaker Switches

Although breaker boxes come in many different styles, one thing they have in common is that when a circuit overloads it trips a toggle switch. The tripped toggle will typically flip all the way off or to a center position. Some designs have a red indicator on the side of the toggle that is visible when the toggle is tripped; with others you have to look for the toggle that's out of line with the rest of the toggles.

Some designs will let you reset the breaker by simply pushing it to the "on" position, while others require you to push the toggle to the "off" position first, and then to "on." If the breaker keeps tripping when you try to reset it, then you'll need to troubleshoot the problem as outlined for fuses above.

If after troubleshooting, the breaker won't reset when you push the toggle to "on," it's possible that you have a faulty breaker. To replace the breaker switch simply:

1.   Cut off the power at the main disconnect.

2.   Remove the screws that connect the panel cover to the box and remove the cover.

3.   Loosen the screw and disconnect the black wire connected to the faulty breaker.

4.   The breaker may have a screw that holds it in place. If so, remove the screw and the breaker should come out easily. Sometimes breakers that have been in for a long time tend to stick and you may have to tap on it with a screwdriver to loosen it.

Some breakers have a clip instead of a retaining screw. In that case, pull the breaker toward you and it should come free. If it's a close fit, you may have to lightly pry the breaker free with a screw driver.

5. Take the faulty breaker to a electrical supply or hardware store and get an exact match.

6. Install the new breaker, flip the toggle to the "off" position, and re-place the panel.

7. Turn on the main disconnect and flip the new breaker toggle to "on." If it snaps off, you've still got an serious electrical short on that circuit and you'll need to call a professional electrician to track down the problem.

As you replace a few switches, outlets, and do some troubleshooting, your confidence and knowledge of your home's electrical system will grow and you'll also save quite a few bucks. Check out the info on the websites listed in this chapter and you can soon add fixtures and additional circuits on our own. For more complicated electrical problems hire an electrician.

HOW TO FIND AN ELECTRICAL CONTRACTOR

If your home's electrical system needs upgrading, it's important that it's done according to the national electrical code (NEC) or your local electrical codes. Yes, you can cut costs by having your brother-in-law, who got a C in high school shop, to do the work. But in the long run that can come back to bite you. How?

1. If the wiring wasn't up to code and you have a fire, it could affect your insurance settlement.
2. When you decide to sell your home, the home inspector, appraiser, or lender may require copies of permits, inspections, or work orders.
3. Substandard wiring can prolong a sale, kill a sale, or force you to reduce your asking price—often by more than what it would have cost you to do it professionally in the first place.
4. Electrical wiring isn't something you cut corners on. You and your home's safety are too important.

The first step to finding a electrician or contractor is ask around for refer-rals, and check with contractors, building inspectors, and Realtors. The goal is to end up with a short list of three contractors (licensed electricians) who will look at your home and give you a detailed written bid.

Incidentally, one way to cut costs is to find a licensed electrician (verify they have a current and active license) who works for a contractor, builder, or even an inspector, and who does jobs on the side for a little extra income. But hiring one of these people doesn't mean you cut down on the detailed paper-work. As with any business deal, the paperwork is your only protection.

No matter whom you hire, here is a list of items you need to have in writing:

- A detailed written description of the work agreed upon.
- An itemized list of materials to be used: number and cost of outlets, receptacles, wiring, breaker boxes, and so on. You can also have the electrician give you a list of materials, which you can then buy. That way you pay for installation only, control the quality and cost of mate-rials, and always know you aren't being overcharged.
- A beginning date and completion date on the paperwork.

Never pay for the job up front. If it's an extensive remodel, you may want to set up a payment schedule as certain parts of the job are completed.

Finally, check with your homeowner's insurance agent and make sure you're covered in case the electrician or any helpers are injured on your prop-erty.

*   *   *

To wrap up this chapter, check the guide in Table 1-2 when you have an electrical problem. Electrical components wear out, malfunction, and are misused. Unfortunately the potential for serious injuries or worse is high, so it's important to stay of top of problems and correct them as soon as possible.

Table 1-2. Electrical troubleshooting guide.

Homes older than 15 years	Get an inspection by an licensed electrician or electri-cal inspector.
Any arcing, sparking, or smell of burning insulation	If it's outside the house, call the power company fast. Inside, cut the circuit disconnect. If you don't know which circuit, flip the main disconnect. Call an electri-cian to check the wiring.
Lights flicker and the TV screen distorts, especially during bad weather.	Could be a bad connection where power comes into the electrical service entrance. Call the power company immediately.
Fuse blows or breaker trips on a circuit.	Check and see what appliances or extension cords are on that circuit and make sure you haven't exceeded the wattage capacity. Inspect the wiring if possible for damaged wiring.

Circuit capacity	15-amp circuits can carry about 1500 watts. 20-amp kitchen circuits can carry about 2000 watts. Add up the wattage of appliances on circuit and take care not to run appliances with too high wattage simultaneously.
One appliance repeatedly blows fuse or trips breaker	The appliance is probably defective, don't use. Repair or replace.
Switch, light, or receptacle blows fuse or trips breaker when use.	Isolate what's on the circuit and check each item for damage. Replace after cutting off main or affected circuit disconnect.
Overamping a circuit.	Never use a higher amp fuse than the circuit is rated for. Example: Using a 20-amp fuse in a 15-amp circuit is a deadly problem waiting to happen.
Lamps or lighting fixtures are overheating or show signs of heat discoloring.	Check the light bulb for too high wattage for the fixture. Example: 100 watt bulb in 60 watt lamp. Match the fixture to the correct bulb. Recessed lighting may have too much insulation and heat can't dissipate; call an electrician to check recessed lighting problems.
You get a shock touching a metal faceplate of an outlet or switch, a lamp socket, or a metal part.	Cut off the circuit and look for a short or miswire in the receptacle or lamp. If you can't locate the problem, check with a qualified electrician.
Receptacles or switches feel hot when touched.	You may have more power than the circuit is designed for. Check the fuse for too high amp rating for circuit. Also, check for loose connections. Call a electrician if it isn't a fuse or connection problem.
Aluminum wiring.	Have an electrician make sure compatible connections are used in outlets and switches. Incorrect connections have caused fires.
You get a shock when touching the outside of metal appliances.	Your wiring system or appliance may not be grounded. Call an electrician ASAP. Shorts and grounding problems are dangerous.

CHAPTER 2

MAINTAINING AND FIXING YOUR HOME'S PLUMBING SYSTEM

In this chapter you'll learn:

- ✓ How your plumbing system works.
- ✓ What problems you can solve on your own.
- ✓ What problems are best handled by a professional plumber.
- ✓ How to upgrade your plumbing system. What pays, what doesn't.
- ✓ How to solve problems using the Troubleshooting Guide at the end of the chapter.

Along with the home's electrical system, plumbing ranks near the top of homeowner's and homebuyer's concerns. But the good news is there's much you can do on your own to fix and maintain your home's plumbing system. You can save a lot of money on service calls and take care of many problems fast without calling a plumber.

Your home's plumbing system is not that complicated; it's just a matter of taking the time to understand how it works and what components tend to wear out. In fact, if you can stand on one foot and pat your head at the same time, you can handle most of the plumbing problems that occur.

Also important is that upgrading and keeping your plumbing system in good condition will make a big difference when you sell your home. And this chapter shows which improvements give you the best return.

Basically, your home's plumbing system is a fairly simple dual system. One part handles water under pressure coming into the home from a municipal system or private well. Components of this part are:

- Your home's supply line, main shutoff valve, pressure regulator, and water meter that ties into the city water main. If you have a private well, the main supply line connects to the well's pressure tank instead of the city water main.
- Cold water pipes that supply water to faucets, toilets, washer, and other appliances on the system.
- The faucets and valves that control water flow until you need it.
- Typically a ³/₄-inch pipe supplies cold water to the water heater. From the water heater, ¹/₂-inch hot water lines supply faucets, dishwasher, washer, showers, tubs, and wherever else you have hot water. In Figure 2-1 the dashed lines are cold water pipes and the solid lines are hot.
- If the city water pressure is over 100 pounds per square inch (psi), a high pressure regulator—usually near the turnoff valve— reduces it to less than 80 psi.
- Of course, for city water the water meter records the number of gallons you use during the billing period. If you forget to pay the bill, the city can shut off the water at the main turnoff, usually located in the street or parking strip.

MONEY-SAVING TIP

Read your meter monthly and keep track of the gallons used. This ensures the water company doesn't make a mistake at your expense. Also, if a water line leaks or breaks, you'll know it before you get hit with a huge bill.

The other part, called the DWV (drain, waste, vent) system, is gravity powered and removes water and waste from the home to a municipal sewer system or private septic system. Its main components are:

Figure 2-1.

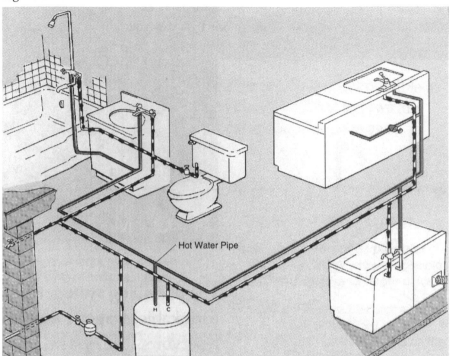

Hot Water Pipe

- 1½-inch to 1¾-inch drain pipes that carry wastewater from fixtures to the 3-inch or 3½-inch diameter, plastic or cast-iron main soil stack that connects to the city sewer or private septic system.
- Drain or "U" traps that connect to the drains of all fixtures. Figure 2-2 shows how these connect to the main soil stack. Drain traps are necessary on all fixtures that connect to a drain because they trap water in the bottom of the U. This creates a water seal that prevents sewer gas (very bad smelling) from leaking into the home and spoiling your dinner party.
- When water moves through a pipe it creates a vacuum and wouldn't flow efficiently if there weren't vents to let outside air into the system. The main soil stack creates one vent, but other secondary vents are needed for each branch that connects to the main stack. Figure 2-3 shows the roof of a typical home where several branch drains vent through the roof.

Once you have an idea of how your home's plumbing system works, regular maintenance will keep it working smoothly and save big bucks on service

Figure 2-2.

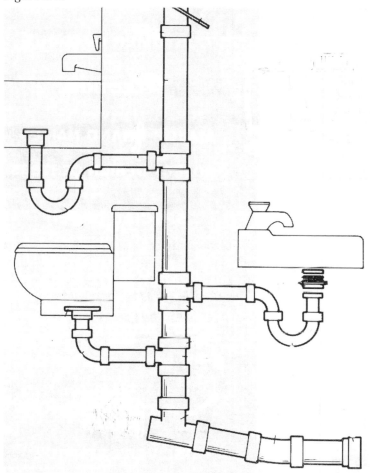

calls. The next section will detail how the supply system works and how to maintain it.

YOUR HOME'S WATER SUPPLY SYSTEM

As mentioned previously, water under pressure piped into your home usually comes from a municipal source or a private well. If you buy water from the city, a branch pipe delivers it from the main water line to your service entrance, which includes a shutoff valve and a water meter.

Just as the main switch cuts off electrical power to your home, as we dis-

Figure 2-3.

cussed in Chapter 1, the service entrance gate valve cuts off water flow to your home. The main water valve is usually located close to where the branch pipe connects to the main. In cold climates, the water main and service lines are buried several feet underground below the frost line. The turnoff valve is typically located at the bottom of a round pipe fitted with a metal cap.

USEFUL PLUMBING WEBSITES

www.hometime.com/Howto/projects/plumbing/plum_7.htm
www.doityourself.com/scat/plumbing
www.allabouthome.com/directories/dir_plumbing.html
www.friendlyplumber.com/plumbing101.html#septic%20system

In most homes, there are also shutoff valves to all the sinks, toilets, and faucets. However, on some older water systems the main valve is the only way to shut off the water.

If your home has only one shutoff valve, updating the plumbing system and bringing it up to code should be at the top of your improvement list. In most areas, these upgrades will increase your home's value by more than the cost of your investment.

One important plumbing item is faucets. Upgrade them or keep them in good leak-proof condition—not only to save water and keep it from staining sinks, but to enhance your home's value.

FAUCET SAVVY 101

Many new homeowners feel that fixing or replacing leaking faucets is something you have to call a plumber for, with credit card in hand. Actually, you can do it yourself. It's not that difficult, all you need is a few tools and a PMA (positive mental attitude).

For starters, plan a shopping trip to your favorite hardware store or home center to pick up a few tools that you may not have. If you're unsure, ask someone in the plumbing section to help you select the right tools. The list should include:

- Adjustable or slip joint pliers, regular and needle-nose pliers.
- An 8-inch or 10-inch adjustable wrench.
- Set of screw drivers that has both flat and Phillips head blades.
- Basin wrench. This is a must-have tool for turning nuts that hold faucets to sinks. It looks like a metal bar with a swivel head and jaws on one end and a slip bar on the other to give you leverage turning the nut. In Figure 2-4 the length of the tool in the foreground adjusts to allow it to fit into tight places.
- Set of Allen, or hex-head, wrenches. These are small, L-shaped, six-sided wrenches that fit Allen or set screws found on faucet handles.
- If you have an older home with separate handles for hot and cold water, you'll need a valve-seat wrench. These look like oversized Allen wrenches with slightly tapered ends to remove valve seats.
- In areas where water has a high dissolved-mineral content (hard water), handles can almost bond to valve stems. So rather than force the handle off the stem and damage it, use an inexpensive screw-type handle puller to break it free.
- Utility knife and extra blades.

Figure 2-4.

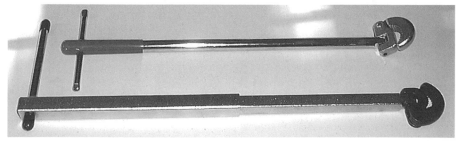

This is a basic set. However, you may need a few other tools depending on the faucet types you have in your home.

> **DECORATING TIP**
>
> If you are renovating an older home or are remodeling, pick out a quality manufacturer, such as Moen, Delta, Peerless, or American Standard. Go with a specific line or style to ensure that all faucets are similar. This will help tie the home's décor together and make it more attractive.

Fixing the Five Most Common Faucet Types

Before fixing a faucet, don't forget to first turn off both hot and cold water lines to the sink.

1. *Two-Handled Faucets.* Two-handled faucets are commonly equipped with washers (compression style) or ceramic stem cartridges; you'll know which type when you disassemble them. If you live in a hard-water area, the seats and washers will need replacing more often than a soft-water area. To fix a compression-style faucet:

   a. Pop the cap off the top of the faucet handle (on some models the screw may not be covered with a cap) with the tip of a utility knife to access the handle screw.

   b. Remove the screw and pull off the handle. If the handle is corroded and won't come off easily, use a handle puller.

   c. Use an adjustable wrench to loosen the stem retaining nut and remove the stem (see Figure 2-5).

   d. On the bottom of the stem is a rubber washer retained by a screw. Replacement kits usually contain two washers, brass screws, and rubber O-rings. First time around, you'll probably need to take the stem to a plumbing supply for a correct match. If the stem is badly worn, replace it too. When replacing the stem and seat, take care not to over tighten.

   e. Another part you'll probably need to replace is the valve seat, especially if you have hard water. Hard water under pressure can cut a small U in the seat causing a steady drip. The valve seat has threads like a screw, so you'll need to use a special tool—a valve seat wrench—to remove it (see Figure 2-6).

Figure 2-5.

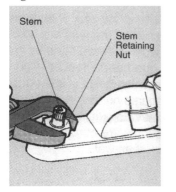

Figure 2-6.

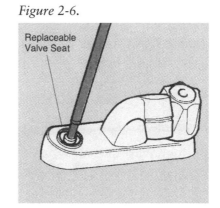

f. Reassemble the faucet with the new parts and test. If the faucet is worn or corroded, you're probably better off replacing it.

2. *Ceramic-Disc Faucets.* Ceramic-disc faucets consist of a cylinder with a moveable disc that rotates to control the hot and cold water mix. In this type, the seals wear and allow the faucet to leak. To disassemble and replace the seals:

a. Remove the small set screw in the handle—it will likely take an Allen wrench or a small flat-head screwdriver.
b. Next, unscrew the cap that houses the cylinder and disks.
c. Remove the screws holding the cylinder in the faucet body and pull out the cylinder. Use pliers if it sticks.
d. Turn the cylinder upside down, remove the seals, and clean the base and seats.
e. Install new seals and reassemble. You may have to take the old seals to a plumbing supply store or home center to ensure the right match.

3. *Ball Type with One Handle.* These faucets are usually inexpensive, and sometimes it's better to replace such faucets rather than try to fix them. However, if you think the faucet is worth fixing you can buy repair kits. To repair, remove the set screw in the handle to access the faucet parts. When you dissemble it, note how the parts fit. Replace the old parts with those in the kit (including the O-rings) and reassemble.

4. *Tipping Valve, Single Handle.* The heart of this faucet is a cam that rotates when you turn the handle, allowing the hot or cold side to open and

close. These are reliable designs, but sometimes particles stick to one of the seats, causing a drip. So before grabbing the pliers, try flushing the problem away by opening and closing the faucet quickly a few times. If this doesn't work, the problem is likely damaged valve seat. To access the seat:

    a. Start by unscrewing and removing the spout. Take care that you don't scar the spout with the pliers when unscrewing the base. Putting masking tape on the pliers jaws can help prevent this.

    b. With the spout off, remove the cover and you'll see a slotted nut on each side of the faucet body. Remove the nut and you can pull out the valve. If the valve is corroded, replace it; otherwise replace the seat only. You may want to take the valve assembly to a plumbing supply store to get the right parts. Also, replace the O-ring on the base.

    c. Screw the base back into the faucet body and the leak should be no more.

    5. *Cartridge Style with One Handle.* This type is sometimes more difficult because the retaining clip holding the cartridge in the faucet is harder to find. It may look like a small ridge projecting out of the exterior under the handle. Needle-nose pliers are the tool of choice to pull it out. You may also have to pop a cap off the top of the handle to remove a screw that holds the handle on. Once the handle is off, you can find the retaining clip that holds the cartridge in. Take the old cartridge to a plumbing supply store for the right match.

    These faucets are some of the more common types, but if you have one that is different, don't panic. The basics are similar: 1) Find the screw that retains the handle and remove to get to the inside. 2) Remove the stem or cartridge and replace along with any O-rings or seats.

    If you decide to replace an old or ugly faucet rather than fix it, the next section tells how.

INSTALLING A NEW FAUCET

Of course, before installing a new faucet you need to remove the old one. Sometimes this is the hardest part of the project, because mounting and coupling nuts that connect faucet to sink are often corroded from being in a humid environment. To find out, look up under the sink with a flashlight and see if there's corrosion, stains, or dirt where the retaining nut threads onto the faucet. If it looks bad, spray the connection with WD40 or another penetrating lubricant and let it set for an hour or so while you catch the game's second half.

After turning off the hot and cold water supply, the following steps show how to remove the old faucet:

1. An adjustable wrench does a good job loosening the water line and faucet mounting nuts if you can get to them. Otherwise, you'll need to use a basin wrench, as illustrated in Figures 2-7 and 2-4. Remember, turn the wrench counter-clock wise to loosen the nuts.

2. If the faucet has a lever that works the pop-up sink stopper, you'll need to loosen the screw that connects the lift rod and pull it out. On kitchen faucets, unscrew the spray hose if it has one.

3. Remove the old faucet and gasket if it has one, and clean up any corrosion or old putty left on the sink.

4. There are two ways to mount the new faucet: 1) Use the gasket that comes with the faucet, or 2) apply a bead of plumber's putty around the base plate's perimeter. In some environments, the gasket may dry out faster than putty, but using the gasket is less messy than spreading a bead of plumber's putty with your finger.

While you've got the water turned off and the lines disconnected, check them to make sure they're in good condition. If not, replace with new braided flex lines and connectors. Also, check the shutoff valves. If they're corroded or the handles are hard to turn, replace them as well. Don't forget to use a turn or two of white Teflon tape on the thread end of metal-to-metal connections. Teflon tape, which comes in small spools, not only helps prevent connection leaks, but it makes connection nuts easier to remove even after years of service. As an alternative to Teflon tape, you can apply pipe joint compound to the threads.

Figure 2-7.

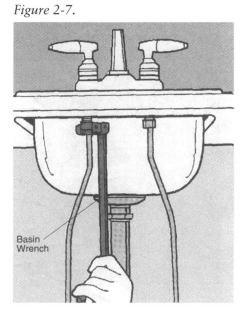

Basin Wrench

When the lines are connected, turn on the water and look for leaks. If you find a connection that's leaking, tighten the nut a little at a time until the leak stops.

TOILET SAVVY 101

No, this section isn't about potty-training kids, which is light-years beyond this home renovator's expertise! But more in the comfort zone is how to keep the potty functioning smoothly, and how to replace parts as they wear out.

HOME VALUE-INCREASING TIP

If you have an older home you're fixing up, start with the kitchen and then next tackle the bathrooms. Make all the bathroom fixtures match so you create a flow. Try not to have mismatching toilets or faucets.

Fixing or keeping toilets in good condition is not difficult. But it's important to stay on top of problems and do as much preventive maintenance as possible. Remember, the humid and chemical environment of a bathroom is unfriendly to metal and plastic parts.

Basically, toilets consist of two systems: water under pressure in; water under gravity out. Simple, but it all has to work together to get the job done. Figure 2-8 illustrates basic toilet design.

Note that a plastic or metal closet flange screws into the wood subfloor and connects to the waste pipe. This provides a solid mounting for the toilet. A very important wax gasket connects the waste pipe to the toilet base. This gasket prevents leaks when the bowl is flushed and water, with the help of gravity, goes down the waste pipe.

Eventually, the wax gasket loses shape or hardens and allows water to escape from under the base. If not corrected, the leak will rot the subfloor. When that happens a section of floor around the toilet will have to be cut out and replaced. This is often the cause of spongy floors in bathrooms and is high on the list of things property inspectors look for. It's also a good reason not to make an offer on a house if you're shopping for one.

Other important maintenance items are the two bolts mounted in the closet flange, shown in Figure 2-8. The toilet base fits over the bolts and is secured by a nut and washer. For cosmetic reasons, a plastic cover hides the bolt and nut.

Figure 2-8.

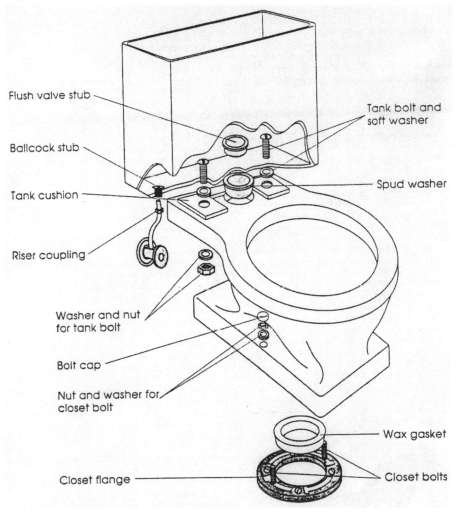

Because these securing bolts and nuts corrode in the humid bathroom environment, you'll want to pop the cap off and check the bolts every few months to make sure they're tight. Loose bolts can also distort the wax gasket and cause leaks.

The water supply is another area of concern. If you need to cut the water supply to the toilet fast, there needs to be a shutoff valve under the tank where the water supply line comes out of the wall.

If there is no valve, hire a plumber to install one. An overflowing toilet can do a lot of damage in the time it takes you to find and cut off the main water supply.

For existing turnoff valves, make sure they turn easily and there are no leaks. If a handle and stem are corroded, replace immediately. These valves are inexpensive and easy to replace. Simply turn off the main water supply, drain the tank, unscrew the water supply line nuts, and remove the old valve. Wrap the threads of the new valve with a couple of turns of Teflon tape and replace.

FOUR WAYS TO LOOSEN A STUCK NUT

1. Tighten the nut slightly. This sometimes breaks the bond between corrosion and nut.
2. Tap the nut with a hammer or punch. Be careful not to damage the threads.
3. Heat the nut with a propane torch or heat gun. Make sure there's nothing flammable close by. Try turning the nut before it cools down.
4. Clean off the corrosion and soak the nut with WD40 if it's rust, or with vinegar if the problem is mostly caused by hard water. Sometimes it takes a day or two of soaking to loosen the hard water buildup.

Two other areas where a leak can happen are the tank mounting bolts and the spud washer that connects the bowl to the tank. If the tank mounting bolts corrode, they can become loose and leak. Loose mounting bolts can also damage the spud washer and leak water behind the bowl. So check the tank mounting bolts every few months to make sure they're in good condition (see Figure 2-8).

If water or a brown waxy liquid is oozing from under the bowl, you probably have a wax gasket that needs replacing. To replace the gasket or closet bolts:

• Turn off the water supply to the toilet and empty the tank by flushing it and sponging up any water remaining in the bottom.

• Disconnect the line either at the turnoff or the bottom of the tank.

• Remove the closet nuts on both sides of the bowl. If they're corroded, use WD40 or a similar lubricant. Tools of choice are a 7/16-inch (or whatever bolt-size you have) boxend wrench or ratchet. An adjustable wrench also works, but you have to be more careful not to round the nut corners.

• Lift the toilet (two people or one NFL linebacker are needed) off the closet bolts and tip it over on its side. Sometimes it's easier to remove the tank first by unscrewing the tank bolts and lifting it off the bowl (see Figure 2-8).

• Remove the old wax ring and clean up the area with a putty knife and rag. Gases from the open sewer line won't be fun to work around, so stuff a rag in the opening—just don't forget to remove it.

• While you've got the bowl on its side, inspect the openings under the rim. This is where water from the tank enters the bowl when you trip the handle. If the openings are restricted by grime or hard water buildup, the flushing action won't be optimum. Use a narrow putty knife, Scotch-Brite pad, and vinegar or other mineral dissolver to thoroughly clean the openings. In areas of hard water, this can be a reoccurring maintenance problem.

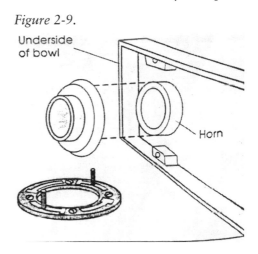

Figure 2-9.

Underside of bowl

Horn

• Install the new wax or rubber gasket and reseat the bowl (see Figure 2-9). Tighten the closet bolts until you feel light resistance; go another turn and stop. The nut should be snug, but not too tight.

Reassemble the bowl and tank, connect the water line, and it should work like new.

DIY PLUMBING WEBSITES

www.toiletology.com
www.stemdoctor.com/toilet_repairs.htm
www.fluidmaster.com/usa.html
www.hometips.com/content/toilets_intro.html

MAINTAINING THE WATER IN-TAKE

The next area of irritating toilet malfunctions is the water in-take system that fills the tank and releases it to flush the bowl (see Figure 2-10). Common problems are:

1. Water continues to trickle into the bowl after the flush cycle. This is often the result of a deteriorated or misaligned flush valve (rubber ball or flap-

per that seals the valve seat). Check and make sure it's aligned for a good fit with the valve seat. If the valve is old or deteriorated, replace it.

2.   The valve seat may be dirty and not allow the flush valve to form a water tight seal when it drops down after the tank starts to refill after a flush.

Figure 2-10.

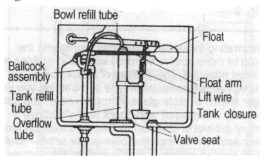

Try emptying the tank and cleaning the valve seat with vinegar. If the problem persists you'll need to replace the valve seat. To do this, turn off the water and disconnect the water line. Remove the two bolts that hold the tank to the bowl (Figure 2-8). Use a spud wrench (available at home center plumbing sections) to unscrew the valve seat (see Figure 2-11). Replace both the seat and washer and reassemble.

3.   Water into the tank doesn't shut off. When the tank empties after a flush, the ballcock or float travels upward as the water level increases. When

Figure 2-11.

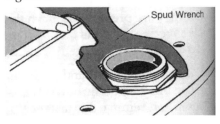

the water level nears the top of the tank, the lever attached to the float shuts off the water with a plunger valve. If this valve malfunctions, water will continue to run into the tank by way of the overflow tube. Worn out seals inside the valve can be replaced, but if it's an old unit, it's better to replace it than try to track down replacement parts.

Replacement is easy: Simply turn off the water and empty the tank. Then remove the ballcock assembly by undoing the retaining nut on the bottom of the tank, disconnecting the chain to the plunger valve and lifting the unit out. At the home center, you'll find several different replacement types at different prices. They'll all work, but get an employee to explain the different models and pick the one you like best. It's just like shopping for jeans.

4.   The tank doesn't empty completely. This is often caused by the chain that raises the flush valve having too much slack. Shorten the chain and flush the tank to see if this solves the problem. You may have to try a couple of chain length adjustments to get it right.

In some areas with high humidity, a toilet tank filled with cold water can sweat enough water to do serious damage to floor and walls. There are two ways to solve this problem:

- *First Option*: Buy a toilet tank insulation kit and install it on the inside of the tank, or try an external cover that insulates the cold tank from the moisture laden air.

- *Second Option*: Have a professional plumber run a water line from the hot water tank to the back of the toilet where it and the cold water line are connected to a mixing valve that brings water up to room temperature before it enters the toilet tank.

True, the second option is a more expensive way to go, but if sweating is a big problem it's cheaper than replacing the subfloor every few years.

It also helps to have a ventilation fan that vents humid bathroom air to the outside. Incidentally, make sure fans don't vent into the attic. You don't want humid air transferring problems from the bathroom to the attic or anywhere else.

After toilets, the next important area that you need to be proactive on are the pressurized water supply pipes and the waste-removal pipes. If you have a home that's older than twenty years, it's important to inspect the plumbing system at least once a year for potential problems.

PIPES: CARE, CLEANING, AND CLOGS

Where water is piped under pressure, Murphy's Law applies: Anything that can go wrong will. Take a proactive approach to keeping your plumbing system in good condition.

If you live in an area with cold winters that freeze pipes, extra care is needed to prevent potentially expensive problems. Many new homeowners move in during warm months, and no one tells them what below freezing temperatures can do to their water system in the months to come. So, here are a few tips on how to keep your pipes from freezing.

- Unheated basements and crawl spaces are prime candidates for cold-snap problems. Possible solutions are:

1. Wrap the pipes with insulation strips or use foam tubes that slip over the pipes.

2. Install a thermostatically controlled space heater.
3. Wrap pipes with electrical heat tape. Install a dedicated outlet rather than running an extension cord.
4. Install a small vent from your home's heating ductwork.

• Pipes that pass through outside walls are especially vulnerable to freezing. They need to be insulated with foam or insulation blown into the wall around the entry area. Using heat tape in addition to insulation is a good idea, especially if the outside wall faces north or is exposed to direct cold winds.

• For outside spigots, install a turnoff far enough into the basement or crawlspace to protect it from freezing. You can then turn off the water and drain the pipe from the turnoff to the outside spigot.

• Pipes that run up or along exterior walls need to be protected by having a professional insulation company insulate the entire wall. A split or frozen pipe inside a wall during a cold snap is guaranteed to cost you pain and big bucks.

In the event you do get a frozen pipe, warm up the frozen section with a hair dryer or heat gun. Have someone stand near the water turn off in case the pipe has a split and you need to cut off the water fast. If you're not sure exactly where the frozen spot is, feel along the pipe until you come to a cold spot and heat that section. If the water stars flowing, you've guessed right. Of course, it's best not to let pipes freeze, because weakened joints or sections can and do develop leaks at the most inopportune time.

Winterizing the Pipes

Winterizing or draining the pipes is critical if you're closing up a vacation home for the winter or planning to be gone from your home for more than a couple of weeks during cold weather. Leaving a home unattended for very long can have serious results if there's a power failure and the furnace shuts down. Some winterizing tips are:

• Drain the water at the lowest point in the system or as close to the main shutoff valve or pump as possible after you've turned off the water where it enters the house or at the street turnoff.
• Turn off the water heater. For gas units, turn off the main gas shutoff on the meter. Electric units can be disconnected at the fuse or breaker box. Drain the tank or the holding tank on a well.

- Open all faucets indoors and out, and empty the toilet tanks of all water. Since there's water left in the toilet S traps, pour a couple of cups of automotive antifreeze into the bowl. Make sure some of the antifreeze spills or flushes into the S trap.
- Outdoor spigots may have knobs that when loosened allow trapped water to drain.
- Pour a cup of antifreeze into all the drains in the home. Don't forget the less obvious ones, such as floor drains or washing machine drain.

Some homeowners like to hire a professional to blow out all the drains with air pressure so there's no water left in the system to freeze. This is the best solution if the home is going to be left unattended for several months of cold weather.

Water Hammer

Water hammer is a common annoyance homeowners experience when water is turned off by a dishwasher, washer, or even a spigot. This loud noise is caused by a lack of air chambers to cushion water under pressure when it's turned off.

Air chambers are short extensions (12 to 18 inches) of capped pipes that are installed in the water line. These extensions contain an air bubble that cushions water in the pipe when it's abruptly turned off. If there's no cushion, flowing water can recoil with a loud bang when you turn it off abruptly. Look at your water pipes and see if you have these extensions.

Some older homes don't have air cushions, but they can be added by cutting the line and fitting a T joint with the capped extension. Unless you're handy with a propane torch, this is a project for which you may want to hire a plumber. Also, your water system may have the extensions but one or more pipes may have lost their air bubble.

If you have this problem, try turning off the water at the main cutoff and allowing the system to drain. Hopefully, the water trapped in the air chambers will drain too. Turn the water back on, and as the pipes fill, air in the extensions should compress to restore the cushion.

Clogged Pipes and Drains

Clogged pipes and drains are the bane for many homeowners, and it can get expensive calling a plumber every time you have a clog. Luckily, there are several things you can do to solve these problems.

The first and most important thing is prevention. Sink drains are designed to handle liquids. But when hair, soap particles, food scraps, and greasy products are carelessly washed into the drain, they often accumulate until they form an obstruction. When this happens you can try a chemical additive that may dissolve the clog, but if that fails, more aggressive action is needed. Some suggestions are:

- Start with a plunger. Block all openings, such as overflow drains or the second drain hole of a double sink, with a rag. (If a dishwasher drains into the sink, disconnect and block that drain as well.)
- Spread a thin layer of petroleum jelly on the rim of the plunger for a better seal.
- Fill the basin with about three inches of water and place the plunger's rubber cup over the drain.
- Push down on the plunger with forceful downward strokes to create a pulse of water that hopefully will break up the clog.
- If the drain clears, run hot water down it for about a minute to clear out all the residue.

Suppose you plunge away for twenty or so strokes and nothing happens, what then? The next step is to remove the U trap under the sink, because these can be notorious clog sites that defy a plunger.

To remove the trap, slip pliers are the tool of choice. Put a bucket under the trap and unscrew the nuts a few turns until the trap slips off the drain tube.

Clean the trap out (a wire coat hanger works great) and remove all the grime with a stiff brush. Heavy deposits sometimes build up on the inside of U traps (especially metal ones) and create rough spots that trap hair, soap scum, and other goop. When this happens, it's better to replace it with a new PVC trap. Take the old one to a plumbing supply and match it up.

Figure 2-12.

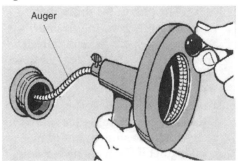

When you take the U trap off and find that it's not the culprit, the clog is probably further into the waste pipe. You'll then need to escalate your attack with an auger (see Figure 2-12). Augers are inexpensive and available at home centers or plumbing supply houses. If you have frequent clogs, an auger that attaches to an electric drill is a good investment.

If the auger fails to restore water flow, the clog is more serious and you'll need to find your credit card and call a professional. With older homes especially, buildup over the years can create choke points where clogs often occur. If your home has these, it's a good idea to replace that pipe section or run an auger through it regularly to prevent problems.

Toilet Clogs

Toilet clogs can be a real pain, especially when small children have tossed things into the bowl. Some suggestions are:

- First try using a plunger with an extended rubber flange that creates a good seal with the trap.
- Empty the bowl of water and use a small mirror and flashlight to see if a toy, hair spray cap, or other item is lodged in the trap.
- If there's nothing caught in the trap, use a plumber's snake or closet auger (flexible auger) to try and remove the clog.
- Still clogged? Then more drastic action is called for. Remove the toilet bowl and turn it upside down. (How to remove the bowl is explained earlier in the chapter) Yes, you'll feel foolish when a toy or plastic cap falls out. A proactive approach to prevent this is keep the lid down so items don't get knocked into the bowl.

Sometimes the problem is in the pipe between your waste system and the main sewer line in the street or the septic tank in the back yard, and replacing it is expensive. In this case, hiring a plumber to clean that section every so often is the most economical way to go.

Because tree roots that invade the waste line as it runs from your home to the main line in the street can create a reoccurring problem, it's a good idea to identify the route your waste line takes across your yard to the main sewer connection and not plant trees near that route.

On the day she moved into her new home, one homeowner had a backup in the basement caused by roots having invaded the line and creating a bottleneck. The offending tree in the front yard had been cut down a few years prior, but the roots that had infiltrated the line had remained, partially blocking it. No one suspected the problem existed until the new homeowner turned on all the spigots in a bathroom at once to flush out the drain. Normally, this shouldn't cause a problem, but in this case the partially blocked sewer pipe backed up, filling the finished basement with a foot of smelly water.

Luckily, the new owner had a good homeowner's policy that covered the cost for a clean-up company to repair the damage.

UPGRADING YOUR PLUMBING SYSTEM

If you have an older home with galvanized or copper pipes, and you want to upgrade or add on, there's some good news. Plastic flexible and rigid pipe, along with simpler ways to attach fittings, make upgrading easier and cheaper than ever.

For example, one homeowner who upgraded the plumbing on his 1971 ranch opted to go with a manifold system. With this type of system, water from the city or pump supply is connected to a manifold, or "switch box." From the manifold, flexible water supply lines branch out to the various faucets, toilets and appliances (see Figure 2-13). Each line has a shutoff; red shutoffs are hot water lines and blue shutoffs are cold. The system has the look of an electrical breaker box.

This brings up an obvious question: If you spend the bucks to upgrade your plumbing, what's the payback when you sell? Of course the real estate market is not the same in all areas, but this is one upgrade that should give you an above average return.

If the upgrade is part of a well-thought-out remodel, it should return above 90 percent in most areas. There's also the indirect return that if the plumbing is not upgraded, the home will sell for less and stay on the market longer. The

Figure 2-13.

bottom line is that in most cases, upgraded electrical and plumbing systems will pay back the investment and often more.

Also, keeping the plumbing system in good working order is critical to maintaining your home's value. In one case, a couple made a full-price offer on a home because it was in an area and of a style they wanted badly. When the home inspection report came back a few days later, the inspector noted that a downstairs bath didn't work. The previous winter a water pipe that supplied the downstairs bath had frozen and created a minor flood in the finished basement. The homeowner's insurance paid to fix the water damage and replace the carpeting, but the sellers capped the pipe rather than replace it.

There were also a few other deferred maintenance items that the buyers would have ignored, but the unresolved water supply pipe problem created in the buyer's minds a what-other-problems-have-the-owners-ignored thinking mode. Since the offer was subject to a satisfactory inspection, the buyers decided to back out of the deal.

Plumbing is an emotional thing with many buyers, more so than carpeting, paint, décor, and landscaping. When they find something leaking or not working, overall credibility suffers.

In the above case, it would have cost the homeowners less than $150 to replace the pipe. Instead it cost them thousands of dollars because it was weeks before another offer came in, and it was much less than the first. By then, time had run out for the sellers; they had to move and were forced to take the lower offer.

To keep your plumbing in good working order, use the Troubleshooting Guide in Table 2-1 to help you solve most messy problems.

Table 2-1. Plumbing troubleshooting guide.

Problem	Possible Solutions
Faucet drips into the sink.	The seals or cartridge inserts need replacing. Remove and take to a plumbing supply for a match.
Water leaks around the faucet base.	Faucet water supply nuts can be loose, the seal between faucet and sink may need replacing. Inside seals leak.
Low water flow from faucet.	If the faucet has a aerator, make sure the screen is not full of sediment. Check water turn-on-valve and lines from water supply to house for leak.
Water leaks around screw on fittings.	Turn off water supply and make sure threads are coated with pipe joint compound wrap a few turns of Teflon tape on threads and reinstall.

(continues)

Table 2-1. Continued.

Problem	Possible Solutions
Water leaks around copper fitting.	Turn off water and drain pipe. Use propane torch to heat the joint and separate pipes. Clean ends with abrasive cloth, coat with flux, slide pipe into fitting and heat while letting solder melt and run into the joint.
Water leaks from the bottom of water heater.	Check drain spigot to make sure it's closed. Look at the bottom of heater with mirror and flashlight for corrosion. If the heater is 8 years old or older you probably need to replace it.
Toilet sweats from cold water in tank.	1. Get inside tank insulation kit for your toilet model. 2. Best long-term solution is having a plumber install a mixing valve that heats tank water to room temperature.
Water leaks into toilet bowl.	Flush valve seat is dirty or worn out. Rubber flush valve is not sitting directly on valve seat and needs replacing. Float may need adjusting to lower water level so water doesn't flow down overflow tube.
Water leaks from under the toilet bowl.	The seal between toilet and waste pipe needs to be replaced. This is either a wax or rubber seal. Remove toilet from bolts and replace.
Toilet bowl is loose.	Remove the plastic caps that cover the mounting bolts on both side of the bowl. Tighten nuts with wrench (usually 7/16) until snug, but don't overtighten.
U trap under sink leaks.	Try tightening locknuts first (hand tight only). You may have to remove trap and replace the washer that the locknut fits over to create a seal. Do not tighten these locknuts with a wrench.
Water leaks from the tank.	Bolts that hold tank to bowl may be corroded and need replacing, or rubber seal (spud washer) may have failed. Drain tank and check. Also check connection where water supply line connects to the water intake valve.
Water from tank continues to run into bowl after flush.	The rubber flapper or flush valve is not seating. Make sure it's positioned above the outlet. Replace if needed.
Toilet is clogged.	First try a plunger. If that doesn't work, try a plumber's snake or auger. Remove water from tank and check with mirror and flashlight for object that may be blocking opening. Finally, if all else fails remove the toilet, turn it upside down, and clean outlet. From now on keep lid closed to prevent objects from falling in bowl.
Water is slow to drain.	Check vent pipes on roof for obstructions that cut off air supply if you can't locate any clogs in the pipe.
Waterlogged soil in the front yard.	You've probably got a leak in the waterline from the street to your home. Call your water company to locate the line. You may have to hire a contractor to replace the water line.

CHAPTER 3

HOW TO CREATE GREAT-LOOKING
WALLS AND CEILINGS

Your home is one of your biggest investments, and it's important to keep it in top condition and protect it so that its value grows. This chapter shows you how easy and fun it is doing those projects that not only enhance the value of your home, but which make it uniquely yours.

Some of the exciting and important things covered in this chapter are:

✓ How to maintain and repair walls and ceilings
✓ Painting tips and techniques the pros use for outstanding results
✓ How to pick out paint colors
✓ Decorating and money-saving tips with relevant websites for more ideas
✓ Worksheets at the end of the chapter that help you calculate the amount of paint you'll need to complete your project

ALL ABOUT WALL CARE

Walls are important components of your home's interior. They not only divide space, but they say a lot about you and your tastes from the way you decorate.

As visitors enter your home the first thing they zero in on are the walls. If the walls are in good condition, tastefully decorated, and have harmonizing colors, the visitors form a positive first impression, and your decorating reputation skyrockets.

On the other hand, dings, nail holes, door knob holes, bad paint, and chipped corners all lower the value of your home and your morale. If the home is for sale, buyers will form a what-else-is-wrong-with-this-dump mentality, and that's not good for full-price offers.

If you're a new homeowner, you're probably excited about the unlimited decorating possibilities. Even more exciting, there's no landlord to tell you your security deposit is at risk if you act on your artistic impulses. But unless it's a new home, there are probably a few holes and other flaws you'll need to take care of before popping off that first paint can lid.

The next few sections show you how to take care of wall problems, along with painting and decorating techniques the pros use that'll make your home look its best with the least cash outlay.

Anatomy of Walls

Interior walls are typically framed with 2×4 inch lumber. The vertical members, called studs, are spaced 16 inches apart, center to center (see Figure 3-1).

Figure 3-1.

In fact, this is such a universal standard that just about all tape measures have the 16-inch position clearly marked (see Figure 3-2). Sometimes homeowners or unscrupulous contractors try to cut corners and space studs 24 inches apart, but this creates an unsafe and less rigid wall.

Basically, walls come in two types: drywall (sometimes called sheetrock or wallboard) and plaster. In some higher-end homes, plaster can still be the wall of choice, but it takes a skilled crew to install it. You rarely find plaster walls in homes built after sheetrock came along in the 1950s. Sheetrock is much easier, faster, and cheaper to install. It commonly comes in 1/2- or 5/8-inch thick, 4 foot by 8 foot or larger sheets, and installers use battery-powered driver/drills and coarse-threaded drywall screws.

Unfortunately, years ago (during the dark ages of home building) nails were commonly used to hang sheetrock, which over time tended to pop out, creating small, unsightly dimples in walls and ceilings. How to fix these dimples is covered later in this chapter.

Figure 3-2.

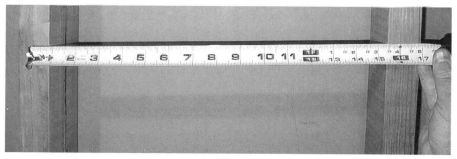

Wall Care

One wall problem is caused by shelves and pictures. It's amazing how often nails are left sticking out of walls when people move out of a home and the new buyer is left with a lot of patch work.

In one case, the sellers had a lot of pictures on the walls, and the home looked great. However, when the buyer entered the home a few hours after closing, she found the walls a mess. Nails were sticking out everywhere, and there were several quarter-sized holes left by wallboard anchors that had been carelessly removed. Also, the previous owners had painted around some of the larger pictures, which when removed left large white rectangles on pale blue walls. Of course, the buyer was upset and angrily called her agent, but the sellers were long gone, and not much could be done about it.

WALL-MOUNTING INFORMATION WEBSITES

www.govart.com/faq.html
www.ab.seweb.uci.edu/FIMA-Picture_safety.pdf
www.ehow.com/how_9936_hang-shelf.html

When mounting pictures, shelves, and other items, it's better to tap wall anchors into a stud rather than into drywall. True, there are wall anchors that work in drywall, but the load limits are small, and if one pulls loose, you've got a sizeable hole to patch.

As for hanging pictures, there are many different choices at your local home center. The key to picking one picture hanging system over another is to think ahead to when you'll need to remove whatever you're hanging. Bigger holes mean bigger patch jobs.

One of the first things many new homeowners want to do before or soon after they move in is paint the interior. Although they have high hopes for great looking walls, too often the results are disappointing. This is usually the result of poor prep work. In many cases, painting can make flaws even more noticeable. The first step in creating a great looking interior is prep the walls by getting rid of dings, holes, popped sheetrock fasteners, settling cracks and uneven spots.

Actually, prepping walls and repairing holes is an important homeowner skill to develop. It's not difficult, it's just a matter of attention to detail and a little practice and your home will always be in top condition.

Fixing Holes, Dings, and Other Repairs

The first step to becoming a drywall ding expert is assembling a tool kit, as illustrated in Figure 3-3. Tools you'll need are:

- 6-inch taping or spackle knives
- Utility knife and spare blades
- Assorted grit drywall sand paper and sanding block
- Drywall screws
- A roll of fiberglass mesh drywall joint tape
- An electric drill with Phillips bit for setting drywall screws
- Premixed all-purpose joint compound (referred to as mud by in-stallers)

Figure 3-3.

- Straight edge
- Claw hammer

A common problem with wallboard in walls and ceilings is that as the house settles, seams open and fasteners pop out just enough to create a noticeable bump. You'll want to correct these bumps before painting or wallpapering.

To repair popped fasteners, first hammer the nail lightly until the head is just below the surface but not breaking the paper wallboard cover. If the fastener is a screw, give it a few turns with a Phillips screwdriver until it's also just below the surface, as shown in Figure 3-4.

Next, drive a drywall screw about 2 inches above or below the popped fastener to keep it from popping out again. If it's loose and the area around it is damaged, remove it. Then cut a length of fiberglass mesh tape large enough to cover both dimples.

> **HINT**
>
> If you're using a cordless drill to set drywall screws, practice on a piece of scrap until you know which setting will set screws just barely below the surface yet doesn't break the paper cover.

Fill the dimples with joint compound and run the flat edge of the trowel over the area to even out the fill. Let the first coat dry and then add another coat. When that coat dries, sand lightly and feather or brush the edges so they blend into the surrounding surface.

Figure 3-4.

To make sure a patched area is completely feathered, hold a bright light next to the repair and look at it from the side. If you see a bump, sand lightly until the surface blends perfectly with the rest of the area. Feathering takes patience and a little practice, but this is critical to ensure that the repaired area doesn't stand out when you paint it.

Small cracks and nail holes can be filled with one or more coats of joint compound as needed and then sanded and feathered. Holes from large nails, drywall anchors and dings can be covered with a piece of mesh tape and two or three coats of compound—and then sanded and feathered, of course.

PATCHING WALLBOARD WEBSITES

www.drywallschool.com/bigpatch.htm
www.thriftyfun.com/tf551724.tip.html
www.wisegeek.com/what-is-drywall.htm
www.alsnetbiz.com/homeimprovement

Bigger holes from doorknobs hitting the wall, moving furniture, and rough-housing kids needs a more aggressive approach. Crisscross the hole with layers of mesh tape and then force joint compound into the mesh with a six-inch trowel and scrape off the excess. Add two more coats and when dry, sand and feather to match the surrounding area.

Another approach on especially large holes, is to cut out the wallboard until you expose half of the stud on both sides of the hole. Cut a piece of wallboard to fit the hole. Secure the patch by driving wallboard screws at each end into the studs; space the screws about two inches apart. Then tape, mud, and sand the seams to blend.

Since you're going to have a bare section of wallboard, you'll need to brush off or vacuum the sanded area to remove dust. Then prime and paint to match the rest of the wall.

Figure 3-5.

Still another hole-patching solution that doesn't require you to cut all the way to the studs on either side is to insert 1-inch by 3-inch furring strips into the hole. The wood strips will extend about two inches beyond the edge of the sheetrock. Drive screws through the sheetrock into the wood strips, giving you a base to pack the hole with joint compound. After the packing dries, cover with mesh tape and add two or three more finishing coats. When dry, sand and feather to match surrounding wall (see Figure 3-5).

DECORATING TIP

Flat paints are more forgiving of wall imperfections but are harder to maintain. Eggshell, satin, and gloss paints are easier to wash but tend to show seams from careless taping and sanding.

Cracks should be filled with mud and sanded. Sometimes it's easier to cut the crack into a V with a utility knife, and then to fill with compound and sand smooth when it dries.

If you've got a really bad wall—with patches, gouges, bad mud, or poor taping—you may want to consider hiring a professional to skim the wall. Basically, the installer applies a thin, even coat of mud over the entire wall. After drying, the wall is sanded smooth and a coat of primer-sealer is applied.

For older homes with plaster walls, fixing a hole is not that difficult. It's a matter of applying several coats of fill, and then waiting for them to dry before applying a final coat of joint compound. The following steps show how:

1.   Scrape and chip all loose material from around the edge of the hole and vacuum.

2.   Undercut the edge of the plaster so it bevels inward towards the metal or wood strips (called lath) that form the backing. This is to create a seat for the patch.

3.   Fill the hole with patching plaster available at home centers. Scrape off any excess and score the patch in a crisscross pattern so the final coat will adhere better and then let dry. The final step is to spread joint compound over the patch and smooth with the flat edge of trowel. Let dry and apply additional coats until the dried patch is roughly even with the rest of the wall. Sand and feather the patch until it's smooth and blends in.

> **ENVIRONMENTAL CAUTION**
>
> Before removing or working with old plaster walls, have a sample tested for asbestos. If the test is positive, contact a licensed abatement contractor for removal and disposal. Because asbestos is a hazardous material, you don't want to breathe in contaminated dust.

Sometimes if the plaster walls are in bad shape, it's easier to hire a professional to install drywall over the plaster.

Water Damage Problems

In one case the homeowners were suddenly awakened by the sound of a huge crash coming from the back of house. Running towards the sound and flipping on lights as they went, the owners came upon a huge mess in the kitchen's dining area. Most of the ceiling had given way and soggy chunks of wallboard covered the table and floor.

For months a yellow stain had spread slowly across the ceiling. Water, which leaked in from a carelessly installed evaporative cooler mounted on the roof, had saturated the ceiling wallboard until it gave way. Luckily, it was in the middle of the night and not during mealtime. What would have been a $10 repair job had now escalated into several thousands of dollars in restoration costs.

Water damage to drywall happens most often to ceilings. A leaking roof or leaking plumbing in upstairs bathrooms are common culprits. Water runs along rafters, or the top surface of the drywall ceiling, until it comes to a seam or corner. Eventually, the water will run down the wall or corner onto the floor.

The first step, of course, is to find the leak and fix it. After that's done, peel away the insulation from the drywall so it can dry out. If the water damage isn't too bad, the drywall may not have to be replaced, although it may have to be refastened and/or retaped and mudded in a few places.

Next, seal the stained areas with an oil-based, stain-covering paint. After the paint is dry, patch with tape and two to three coats of mud. Sand and feather the seams. If no water stains have bled through the covering paint, apply the ceiling top coats.

Another solution is to texture the ceiling with a spray-on or hand-applied finish. These finishes are not only good at hiding minor problems, but create attractive ceilings. There's a wide variety of finishes and patterns available. However, it's probably best to hire a professional to do the texturing; it can be messy.

ENVIRONMENTAL CAUTION

Older "cottage cheese" ceilings sprayed on before 1980 may contain asbestos. The only way to find out for sure is have a lab test. Usually these ceilings are not hazardous to those living in the home. However, there may be some hazard if you remove the finish by scraping it off dry. If the lab test is positive for asbestos, you may want to have a professional remove it especially if all the rooms in your home have that type of ceiling.

After ceilings and walls are in good condition the next step to making your home stand out is a super paint job. Painting is not difficult, and if you can spell your name and write cursive, you can do a top-notch paint job. The next section shows how.

HOW TO CREATE A GREAT PAINT JOB

The joy of living in a well-decorated home, that feeling of pride when company comments on how nice your home looks, and, of course, the boost a great interior gives your market value—these are great reasons to learn how to do a super job with brush and roller.

Painting can be fun and rewarding, especially when it's all done and you step back and see outstanding results. Many people who say they hate painting and don't want anything to do with it may ultimately admit that they once tried to paint a room and it turned out terrible.

Fortunately, terrible paint jobs don't have to happen, and they won't if you learn and apply the easy steps to follow. Admittedly, there's some grunt work involved, but the end result is more than worth the effort.

Actually, a great paint job is one of the easiest and best things you can do to increase the value of your home. If you're thinking of selling in the near future, you'll want to get started on the painting about ninety days prior to planting a For Sale sign, so it doesn't turn into a rush job.

However, if you've just bought a home and are looking at dismal or uninspiring contractor- white walls, this section will show you how to change your environment for the better.

First, plan on about two days per room. No, you can't knock out painting the house over the weekend; not even the Labor Day weekend. Even though slumlords and painters with power sprayers can coat a new house in a day, that's not for you. So allocate the time to do it right, which means a room at a time.

Basically, painting a room consists of three parts:

1. *Prepping the Room.* This encompasses getting the drywall in perfect condition, because a paint job can be no better than the prep work. Remove or mask all the fixtures, doorknobs, and whatever you can't remove from the room.

2. *Priming the Walls.* A great-looking top coat starts with a great primer coat.

3. *Applying the Top Coat.* This is the main event. Using good technique, tools, and paint will guarantee you a lot of compliments at your next party.

The Prep Work

To begin, move everything out of the room, even large furniture. Prep dust, spackle, and paint have little homing devices that target anything left in the room, even when covered in plastic. Also remove doors, light fixtures, and hardware, and then use blue painter's masking tape to mask everything that's left. Table 3-1 at the end of this chapter is a checklist you can use to help you make sure you have the proper equipment on hand as you begin your project.

HOW-TO PAINTING WEBSITES

www.alsnetbiz.com/homeimprovement/painting.html
www.paintingyourhouse.info
www.house-painting-info.com
www.behr.com/behrx/expert
www.thisoldhousepaints.com
www.ppg.com/ppgaf/pittsburgh/ptechniques.htm

Cover the floor with good canvas or paper-backed plastic drop cloths. Avoid old bed sheets or other thin fabrics because paint will easily soak through them. Plastic sheeting provides a good cover, but it is slippery, and spilled paint makes it an even more unsafe working surface.

The next step is to inspect the wall for any holes, cracks, dings, or other problems. Even if the wall looks good, shine a strong light—an old lamp with a bare bulb works great—next to the wall and you'll quickly notice any imperfections.

You can repair damaged woodwork or molding with painter's putty or a wood filler, such as Minwax's High Performance Filler. Both products sand to a smooth finish.

Next, follow these tips to put your walls in painting shape:

• Lightly sand the entire wall to make sure there are no glossy spots.

• Using a soft bristle brush, go over the wall to remove any sanding dust.

• Wash the walls with Trisodium Phosphate (TSP) available at home centers. If smokers live or have lived in the home, use 50/50 bleach and water solution. Use this solution also if you live in a mildew problem area to kill any spores hanging around.

• Unless you're great with a cutting brush, use blue painter's tape to tape the molding and other surfaces you don't want painted. To prevent paint from bleeding behind the tape, run a putty knife along the edge to seal it.

• At any home center or paint store, buy an inexpensive caulking gun and several tubes of latex paintable caulk. Make a diagonal cut to remove about a quarter of an inch from the clear plastic tip of the tube latex—just enough to get a controllable bead. Run the wire attached to the gun down through the tip and puncture the cartridge's seal. Place the cartridge in the gun and squeeze the trigger a few times until caulk starts flowing (see Figure 3-6).

- Run a bead around window and door casings, floor molding and other gaps. Moisten a finger and smooth out the bead so it blends smoothly with the wall surface. If you have old caulking that's in bad shape, remove it with a putty knife and recaulk.

Figure 3-6.

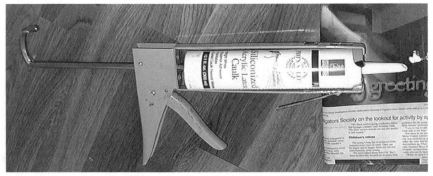

How to Pick the Primer

Primers are formulated to create a solid base, seal stains, and help bond the top coat to the wall. Both alkyd and latex primers give good coverage and do a great job. Which one you choose will depend on the top coat you have chosen.

Also, go with good quality, brand-name primers and paints, such as Sherwin-Williams, Pratt and Lambert, Benjamin Moore, or Pittsburgh Paints. Better yet, go to a professional paint supplier and talk to the knowledgeable employees. They can give you valuable tips and help you get the paint system (primer and top coat) that will work best in your climate and for the job you're doing.

Some important priming tips are:

- If the walls and ceilings have been heavily prepped and the first coat didn't quite do the job and there's a light bleed through, put on a second coat.
- Some climates, especially those close to salt water, need a second primer coat.
- Work closely with your paint supplier. Some primers are better for wetter rooms such as bathrooms and laundries. In other words, one primer doesn't necessarily fit all conditions.

- Older homes that were built without vapor barriers will need a primer that seals and prevents moisture from getting under the paint and causing peeling.
- Drywall and plaster walls are different and usually require different primers. Talk to your paint dealer for the best type to match your walls and conditions.
- Interior wood trim can also need different primers. Your paint dealer can also point you in the right direction in this area.
- If you've primed over unpainted drywall or wood trim, you'll probably need to lightly sand after the primer has dried. Primer tends to raise the fibers or grain so a light sanding is needed before painting the top coat. Be sure to run a tack cloth over the sanded area so no dust is left behind.
- Never spot prime problem areas on walls that you've had to go back and work on. Those areas will often show through. Correct the problems and then recoat the entire wall. Fortunately, ceilings are more forgiving and don't show spot priming as much. There are also special paints formulated for ceilings that cling to textured surfaces better than wall paints. Check with your paint supplier for what works best on your type of ceiling.
- If you're going with a darker top coat, tint the primer coat to match. It may save you having to apply a second top coat.

How to Pick the Top Coat

A trip to the home center or paint supplier can be confusing. There are dozens of paint types, methods of application, and special effects to choose from. The following tips will help you sort out the confusion:

- Go with a high quality latex primer and top coat. That means you'll spend $20 to $35 per gallon. Top quality paint goes on better, lasts longer, and looks better than cheap discount paint. Consider it an investment in your home's value.
- Gloss and semi-gloss paints are more stain-resistant and washable, but highlight any wall problems. Flat paints are great for living and dining rooms. Eggshell gloss is a good all-around finish for hallways, kids' rooms, kitchens, and bathrooms.
- Some pros feel flat paint is the best way to go for ceilings, others like a bright white gloss that reflects more light into the room. If your

home tends to be on the dark side, gloss ceilings reflect more light and makes the room feel larger.

- Plan on two top coats for the best looking job and figure on about 400 square feet per gallon. Also, make sure you have about a half gallon left over for touch-ups.
- If you live in a dry climate, you may want to include an additive to slow down drying time and make the paint more workable. Adding a few ounces per gallon of Floetrol (www.flood.com/Flood/Products/ Interior/PaintAdditives) or another similar additive can make the job go easier.
- Check out mildew-inhibiting paints if you live in a humid area, and also for baths, kitchens, and laundry rooms. These paints will not kill mildew that's already present, but they'll prevent mildew from forming later on.

Worksheet 3-1 is a handy checklist to fill out and take to the paint supplier so you don't forget anything important, and Worksheet 3-2 helps you calculate how much paint you'll need for your project. Both worksheets are located at the end of this chapter for ease in making copies of the forms.

WEBSITES TO HELP YOU CHOOSE PAINT COLORS

www.interiordec.about.com
www.sherwin-williams.com/doityourself
www.paint.org/con_info/choosing.cfm
www.purecontemporary.com/FeatureArticle/article/103
www.architecture.about.com/cs/repairremodel/a/pickcolors.htm
www.home.ivillage.com/decorating/color/topics/0,,4tjs,00.html

---

Once you've decided on the paint system, the next step is to decide on the colors and tints. For some homeowners this is the project's fun part, for others it's divorce material. Luckily, there are six shortcuts that will help you decide:

1. Take your time and check out builder's open houses to get ideas of what's currently trendy in your area.
2. Look at color schemes in home magazines and check out the websites listed in the box.
3. Collect paint chips of colors you like and narrow it down to those that you think will go with your home's other colors.

4. Remember, color choice should take into consideration your home's architecture, ceiling height, and exterior and interior colors.

5. Once you've narrowed it down to three or four colors, get pint samples from the paint store and roll four foot swaths on one of the walls you're planning on painting. Live with it for a couple of days and see which color grabs you.

6. Don't be afraid of making a big mistake. What's the worst that can happen? You can always repaint!

Remember that although this is your home, it's also your biggest investment. At some point you will likely want to sell, either because you're moving up or relocating. The average American only stays in their home seven years. So keep this in mind when you paint. Don't follow the example of two homeowners who painted every room of their home a different bright color: blue, green, salmon, yellow, and pink! The homeowners said they wanted to express their artistic sides and felt confident others would feel the same way and their home would sell fast.

Reality, however was much different. The home sat on the market for months and not even a generous painting allowance stirred up interest. As one homebuyer said after looking at the home, "The owners must think I'm dumb to buy this home and put a huge amount of work into painting it when for the same price I can buy another home that hasn't been ruined."

In the end the home finally sold, but the owners lost many thousands of dollars that investing a few hundred dollars could have prevented. In another similar situation, the owners painted all the rooms in their home a bright fire-engine red. When they needed to sell, the result was almost predictable: The home stayed on the market a long time and ended up selling for a steep discount. Why did these homeowners paint all the rooms red? According to them, "We wanted to be cool and impress our friends. . . ."

The lesson learned here is that if you want to go over the top into bizarre color choices, it's going to eventually cost you. Either you'll have to repaint before selling, or you won't get top dollar. Good taste increases value, non-mainstream decorating will cost you unless you want to do a lot of redecorating when you decide to sell.

So, if you're not confident in your color choices, talk to the people at paint stores the pros use: They know the current trends. Other sources are magazines, builder open houses, and home fix-up programs on TV.

Now that you've got all those buckets of paint lined up on the paint store's counter, the next step is to mosey over to the painting tools section and get the hardware you'll need to do a pro job.

How to Choose the Right Painting Tools

After spending a lot of time and energy prepping the walls and ceilings and buying a top quality paint, you don't want to skimp on the tools that make a super job happen. Many people who hate to paint and decorate developed that attitude because they once tried to paint with poor tools and cheap paint and got disappointing results.

Investing in good quality tools is less expensive in the long run than going with bargain brands that are thrown away after the job is done. Because good tools last for many paint jobs, the cost becomes much less when spread over several redecorating jobs. They also usually help speed up a job. A word of caution: Don't lend your good painting tools to your friends or relatives. You won't get them back!

The tools you'll need are:

- Drop cloths with canvas backing—they absorb paint drops and don't allow paint spills to soak through. Plastic sheeting works, but spilled paint soon makes it slippery and that's a safety concern.
- A couple of 5-gallon buckets. Since colors can vary slightly from gallon to gallon, it's a good idea to pour all the gallon cans into one of the buckets, mix thoroughly, and work from the 5-gallon container (see Figure 3-7).
- Several 2-quart buckets to pour small paint quantities into for brush work.
- A coarse screen that sits inside a 5-gallon bucket to roll excess paint off. Notice that Figure 3-6 shows no roller pan. That's because a shal-

Figure 3-7.

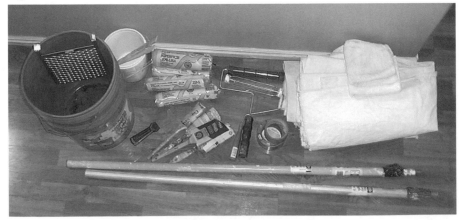

low pan is easier to spill, easier to put your foot into, and a pain to keep refilling.

- One telescoping pole for each painter. This allows you to do both walls and ceilings without ladders or boxes to stand on.
- Nine-inch rollers are the best all-around size. Get good quality 1/2-inch lamb's wool rollers for walls and ceilings. If you want to cover up some imperfections, a longer nap gives you a slight texture.
- Quality paint brushes are a must. If you must give up lunches for a month to get the best brushes, it's worth it. Get a couple of 2-inch or 2 1/2-inch brushes with angled soft nylon bristles (cutting brushes), and a couple of 4-inch brushes with straight bristles. Also look for tapered bristles with split ends that help work an edge and spread the paint smoothly. Plan on spending about $25 plus for a good brush that can last for a long time.
- Have lots of rags on hand for spills and dabbing up mistakes. Whatever you have around the house works.

Before you start slinging paint, you need to make a decision. Do you want to use a brush to paint the line between wall and ceiling or use masking tape? If you're a newbie to painting, you probably should use masking tape.

MAKE-LIFE-EASIER TIP

You can buy paint at K-Mart, Wal-Mart, and other discount stores, but you don't want your walls to look like blue-light specials, do you? So find out where the pros buy their paint. Look for vans with ladders on top taking up most of the parking places. The people selling paint at these stores know their product and can advise you. You can find them in the phone book under Paint Dealers.

Start with a roll of blue 2-inch-wide painter's tape and go around the room's perimeter with the top edge abutting the ceiling. After the perimeter is taped, run the edge of a spackle or taping knife along the top edge. This seals the tape to the wall so paint won't bleed under the edge.

With all the tools and paint sitting in the middle of an empty room and the wall masked, it's now showtime. The ceiling comes first, and those painting poles are going to earn their keep. However, when you do the brush work around the edges, you'll need a short stepladder or two milk crates and a stout plank.

Painting Techniques: How the Pros Do It

In doing the ceiling, the brush work comes first. Fill a 1-quart or 2-quart container about half-full of ceiling paint to work from. Using a 3-inch or 4-inch brush, dip it about an inch or two into the paint, and tap both sides of the brush against the container side to remove the excess. Start at one corner and lay an even, smooth coat—just thick enough to cover—about 1½-inches wide to the other corner and then on around the room.

Feather the paint towards the middle of the ceiling so you don't get a smooth hatband effect around the ceiling edges. Some pros, however, prefer to roller the ceiling first and then use a brush to paint the half inch or where the roller can't get around the edges. If there's crown molding, do that next. The key is work from the top down.

That's all there is to it; after a while you'll develop a rhythm that makes the work go faster and smoother. As your brush talents develop you may find you can dispense with masking tape and cut a fine line just like the pros.

Once the ceiling's perimeter is painted, slip a roller cover onto the handle and screw it onto a painter's pole. With the 5-gallon bucket about half full of paint and the grid in place, dip about a quarter of the roller into the paint and run it over the grid to work paint into the nap. Cover the ceiling with broad, overlapping strokes, taking care not to leave any ridges of paint. You want to create a thin even coat. Don't try to load up paint to get a one coat coverage—two coats give better looking results.

Once the ceiling coats are dry, lightly run the edge of a drywall knife or spackle knife along the masking tape's paint edge. If you try to rip the tape off without doing this first, you'll pull some of the dried paint with it, creating a ragged edge.

DECORATING TIP

When you choose your paint color, match it to your floor colors, appliances, and furniture. The key to an outstanding home décor is picking a color that runs throughout the house and keying everything else to it. It's like matching up suit, shirt, and tie—or dress, shoes, and purse.

Next in line is crown molding. Tape the wall below the molding using blue painter's tape. A 2-inch or smaller brush works well for painting molding, and use a container that holds about a quart of paint. When the molding is dry remove the tape as before, scoring it along the paint edge before pulling it off.

Walls are next, but before you mask the ceiling make sure it's completely dry. You don't want ceiling paint sticking to the tape when you remove it. Also mask the base molding and anything else that you don't want paint on.

The pole extensions make painting walls a snap. No step ladders or boxes to get in the way, and you can stay far enough way from the wall to spot runs or other problems.

After the first primer coat is dry, give the wall a light test for any irregularities. Then lightly sand the wall with 320 grit sandpaper and remove any dust with a tack cloth. If the wall looks great, roll on the top coat and again give it the light test. Apply the final top coat and let dry before scoring and removing tape.

The last item to be painted in a room is the base molding. Again, you'll need to tape the wall to avoid ruining a great-looking wall.

Window sashes can be a challenge. You need to paint each one with a high degree of control, which using 1-inch brushes allows you to do. As for paint on the glass, you can either tape the panes or scrape off the paint when it dries with a single-edge blade. Doors are best removed to where you can paint or stain them while they rest on sawhorses.

Since painting projects can last for several days, you can put brushes and rollers into a plastic bag, which you can seal and store in the refrigerator between coats. At the end of the project, brushes should be cleaned thoroughly in warm soapy water and hung bristles down to dry. Wrap brushes in old newspaper and store until the next project calls. Roller covers are usually not worth cleaning and can be thrown away.

When painting or repairing your walls and ceilings, use the guide in Table 3-1 to help you solve most problems.

With wall and ceilings in top shape, many homeowners next cast an eye on upgrading their floors, counters, and kitchens. How to do that is coming up in Chapter 4.

Table 3-1. Common wall and ceiling problems and how to solve them.

Problem	Possible Solution
Plaster wall is in bad condition.	Have a professional install drywall over the plaster. After mudding, taping, and sanding the wall, you can paint it. This is often easier than trying patch plaster holes.
Drywall is in bad condition.	If it's just a few dings and holes, they can be patched. If that isn't practical, you can drywall over the existing wall and finish.
Door knob punched hole in wall.	1. You can buy shock absorbers at home centers that mount over the hole and protect it. 2. Use drywall tape to crisscross the hole and then mud, tape, sand, and refinish. 3. Put a wood backing in the home and fill it will compound. Then sand and refinish.
Wall has a lot of shallow dings or an uneven surface.	Hire professional drywall finisher to skim the entire wall with joint compound and then sand it smooth. You may need an extra coat of primer to make the wall look super.
First coat of primer made the wall rough.	On new or poorly painted drywall, the first primer coat often raises fibers in the paper covering. Sand the wall with 220 grit sandpaper, vacuum well or use a tack cloth, and roll on a second coat of primer. That coat may need sanding also.
Prepping walls painted with gloss paint.	Home centers sell liquid deglossers, or you can sand the wall with 220 grit sandpaper and clean off dust with a tack cloth.
Pulling masking tape off the wall tears the paint and leaves a ragged edge.	Whenever you're applying masking tape, run a taping blade over the paint side edge to seal it tightly against the surface so paint won't bleed under it. When you remove tape, run the blade's edge lightly over the same edge to cut the paint-to-tape bridge or bond so the tape will lift of cleanly.
Getting rid of cottage cheese or popcorn ceilings.	If the texture is non-asbestos, you can it spray lightly with water and scrape it off with a wide putty knife. Cover the floor with plastic because there's going to be a big mess. After scraping the texture off, sand smooth and apply a primer coat or two before painting the top coat.

Worksheet 3-1. Painting project equipment checklist.

Tools and Equipment	Have on Hand	Need to Get
1½ or 2 inch trim brushes		
Drop cloths: canvas or paper-backed		
Blue 2-inch masking tape		
Nail set for resetting popped nails		
Lamb's wool roller covers		
Roller handles		
Extension poles		
220 and 320 grit sandpaper		
Sanding pole and sanding blocks		
One gallon of joint compound		
Two 5-gallon buckets		
Painting screens		
Several 2-quart painting buckets		
Caulking gun and paintable caulk		
Rubber or latex gloves		
Wood stirrers		
Joint or spackle knives		
Water bucket and sponge		
A dozen rags		
Small step ladder		

Worksheet 3-2. Job quantity and cost estimator.

Room or Ceiling	Square Footage	Sq. Ft. Divided by 400 = # of gallons	Cost per Gallon $	Total Cost $

Sample calculation:

Room or Ceiling	Square Footage	Sq. Ft. Divided by 400 = # of Gallons	Cost per Gallon $	Total Cost $
Living Room	438 sq.ft.(primer)	2 coats needs 2 gal	$25 × 2 = $50	50.00
	Top coat		$30 × 2 = $60	60.00

Directions for using the cost estimator table:

Suppose you're painting the living room and dining room. The living room walls measure 18 feet × 8 feet for two walls (1 and 2), and 16 feet × 8 feet for the other two walls (3 and 4). There are two doors at 3 feet × 7 feet and two windows at 8 feet × 4 feet each.

Wall 1 = 18 feet × 8 feet = 144 square feet
Wall 2 = 18 feet × 8 feet = 144 square feet
Wall 3 = 16 feet × 8 feet = 128 square feet
Wall 4 = 16 feet × 8 feet = 128 square feet
                      Total = 544 square feet

Less square footage for doors and windows:
    Doors: 3 feet × 7 feet × 2 doors = 42 square feet
    Windows: 8 feet × 4 feet × 2 windows = 64 square feet
    Total to be subtracted = 106 square feet

Square footage to be entered in table is 544 − 106 = 438 square feet.
Estimating 400 square feet coverage per gallon or 438 divided by 400 = about 2 gallons for two coats. By using this formula for each room, and filling in the table, you can estimate what it will cost you to paint the inside of your home.

CHAPTER 4

INTERIOR IMPROVEMENTS
THAT ADD VALUE

One of the biggest and most perplexing challenges for new and even seasoned homeowners is deciding which improvements add value and which ones just end up costing them big bucks.

Basically, home upgrades and improvements can be loosely divided into two areas: those that are needed to maintain the home, and those that are elective and may not return your investment. Sometimes there's a blend, such as an upgrade that returns only a fraction of the cost but one you enjoy while living in the home, and that's payback enough.

Some examples of the first category would be repairing or replacing a roof, furnace, water heater, or carpeting. If you don't make these types of improvements, the home's value and your enjoyment of it suffers. This is why replacing a roof usually doesn't increase the value of your home. Buyers expect a good roof as part of the purchase price.

Elective upgrades are often area specific, in that what is routine in one area may not be so in another. A prime example is Phoenix or Los Angeles, where a swimming pool is almost standard; without one value suffers. In Grand Rapids, Minnesota, a pool would create a hard-to-sell property. There you would need to stay in the home for enough years to make a pool worth the loss when selling.

The key to upgrading and improving your home is knowing what to improve and what may not return your investment. That's the focus of this chapter, as well as the following:

✓   Tips on upgrading floors, kitchens, baths, and other rooms

✓   How to shop for energy efficient appliances and upgrades

✓   How to save money on your upgrades

✓   How to hire and work with contractors and remodelers so you don't get taken.

✓   Useful websites that point you to more specific information

Many new homeowners start out expressing their decorating and artistic talent by painting their walls and ceilings, as was covered in Chapter 3. Once that's done, they often start thinking of upgrading floors. And like choosing paint, flooring options have exploded with exciting choices and new materials. The next section shows how to shop for and pick out what flooring will work best for your home.

MAINTAINING AND UPGRADING FLOOR COVERINGS

Floor coverings are an important part of enjoying your home and maintaining its value. Some types are trendy and exciting, but when after a few years their owners tire of them, they end up in the landfill. Examples of these are avocado, gold, and red long-shag carpets and their matching appliances.

The key to picking flooring is go with a type that has stood the test of revolving-door fads and trends. Oak, for instance, is a classic. Other woods and finishes bubble to the surface for awhile and then fade away, but oak seems to keep coming back because few finishes can match its beauty.

MONEY-SAVING TIP

You can save a lot of money on tile floors if you take a class on tiling from adult education sources, home centers, or tile suppliers. Laying tile is easy and fun, and if you shop around you can find incredible bargains on discontinued patterns, styles, or overstocks.

Basically, floors are covered in either carpet, tile, vinyl, wood, or combinations. You get the best results when matching the flooring material to the room and environment.

Flooring Options for Different Rooms

Starting with kitchens, tile is the number one choice. True, wood looks great in a kitchen and the wood laminates are water resistant. But nothing outwears tile, and you can save a lot of money installing it yourself. There's zillions of patterns, styles, colors, and textures, and they are continually changing. Even more exciting is that you can go with different grout colors to create a truly unique floor.

DECORATING TIP

If you just bought a used home and are planning on fixing it up, paint the house first, then match floor coverings to wall color, and finally choose the furniture, appliances, and accessories to compliment the wall colors.

You can also rent tile cutters and other tools cheaply from most home centers and tile suppliers. If you end up doing a lot of tiling, buying the tools is not that expensive, and it's a good investment because they last a long time. Just don't lend them to your brother-in-law.

Tile is also great for bathrooms, for the same reason it's great for kitchens: it's long wearing, waterproof, big-dog proof, kid proof, and so on. Other great places for tile are laundry rooms, entryways, and borders around family rooms. Developing a pattern or color and carrying that theme throughout all the rooms you tile helps tie your décor together.

Wood floors are so understandably popular that your options can get confusing. Table 4-1 gives some interesting comparisons:

One homeowner had a couple of large dogs that destroyed a vinyl floor and scratched and gouged a natural wood floor. He finally installed a good quality laminate. The dogs can't get traction and they spin out trying to corner on the slick finish, but after two years the floor still looks great. Other homeowners with active pets have also had good results with tile floors.

Table 4-1. Popular wood-floor options.

Type	Pros	Cons	Average Cost
Solid wood	Beautiful looking. Can be refinished numerous times.	Humidity causes floor to expand or contract. Scratches easily with pets.	Plan on $10 to $12 dollars a sq. ft.
Engineered wood or wood veneer over plywood	A huge variety of patterns and styles.	Limited or no refinishing capability.	$8 to $12 a sq. ft.
Bamboo and other eco-friendly species	Natural colors and unusual grain patterns. Durable, attractive and environmentally friendly.	Costs slightly more than other solid wood options.	$12 to $18 a sq. ft.
Previously used or reclaimed wood	Unique features, can be beautifully finished. Environmentally friendly, no trees cut.	More expensive and hard to find. Usually in unfinished boards.	$12 to $28 a sq. ft. unfinished.
Laminates	Easy to install tongue and groove. Economical. Good choice if you have pets.	Cannot be refinished, but a good quality laminate has an extremely durable finish.	$5 to $8 per sq. ft. installed.
Cork Planks	Resilient, durable, easy to install panels.	Not for baths, laundry rooms, or other wet areas.	$3 sq. ft. if you install.

Along with tile and wood floors, carpet is a main-stream floor covering. There's a bewildering array of fiber, colors, and pattern choices. Carpeting, however, isn't for high traffic, wet, or hard use areas, such as entryways, kitchens, baths, and laundry rooms. It works best in bedrooms, living rooms, and family rooms. However, some homeowners like carpeting in hallways and on stairs for its noise-dampening ability.

When you go shopping for carpeting, look for these three characteristics that define quality:

1. *Pile*—the height of the fibers
2. *Density*—how many fibers there are per square inch
3. *Texture*—how the fibers are looped, twisted, or cut

The more dense a carpet is, the longer it's likely to last. As for texture and pile, that tends to be a more individual choice. You run your hand through the samples and narrow it down to the ones you like the feel of.

Nylon is probably one of the best carpet choices, with costs from $12 to $24 per square yard. If you have allergies, wool may be a better choice, although it doesn't do as well in humid climates and its cost is around $25 to $80 a square yard. Still, wool is the fiber all others are compared to. If you have the climate and budget, wool is hard to beat.

HELPFUL FLOOR-COVERING WEBSITES

www.carpetguru.com/const200.htm
www.thisoldhouse.com/toh/knowhow/interiors/article/0,16417,229547,00.html
www.splisc.com/carpet/category_2387.html
www.familyresource.com/lifestyles/home-and-garden/what-to-look-for-when-
    picking-out-a-carpet
www.duro-design.com

Polyester is the at the bottom for durability and cost. It's costs about $8 to $12 per yard. If you go with polyester carpet, get a better quality pad, which means thicker and denser than the usual pad paired with this type of carpet.

There are so many patterns and colors to choose from that it's easy to suffer from sensory overload, but here are some tips to help narrow it down.

- Paint a bold swab of your wall paint on a piece of white paper and take it with you carpet shopping (after it dries, of course).
- If you're leaning toward a patterned carpet, the dominant color should match the wall color.
- For solid colors, you can contrast, compliment, or match. Which way you go depends on your home's architecture, how light or dark it is, and your taste. Darker carpet makes a room look smaller and shows lint and pet hair more than lighter colors. Rooms with lots of windows and high ceilings can go with darker carpet better than a home that doesn't get much light.

- Light carpet colors tend to make rooms look larger, especially if the home is a ranch or bungalow. And if you have a blond Lab, it won't show the pet hair.
- Narrow your choices down and take samples home to see how they match in your house. Showrooms are likely to have different lighting from what your home has, so you need to see what the colors look like in your setting.
- Also keep in mind that you're going to be living with the carpet for a few years, and that classy plaid or bright purple may not be the rage for long. It's better to stay with classic colors and patterns that won't date your purchase.

Decorating your home can be a work-in-progress journey. In reality, that's what makes homeownership fun. You decorate it; if you don't like it you can redo it. You don't have to live with the landlord's decorating!

Once you have the walls and flooring to your liking, decorating the bath(s) to your expectations can do a lot to turn your house into a home. As one new homeowner said when the Realtor handed her the condo keys: "Once I get the bath fixed up the way I want, the rest will fall into place."

MAINTAINING AND UPGRADING BATHS

For many homeowners who have older homes, the bath(s) is one of their biggest maintenance challenges. Leaks, clogs, water damage, and cleaning demand time and treasure to keep them "house guest" clean.

> **MONEY-SAVING TIP**
>
> It's often much cheaper to refinish older tubs than go with a tear-out and replace. Check the yellow pages for companies that refurbish tubs onsite. Two interesting websites on refinishing are:
>
> www.bobvila.com/wwwboard/messages/48204.html
> www.permaglaze.com

Chapter 2 covered how to handle common plumbing problems. This section will cover how to maintain the rest of the bathroom: cleaning, upgrades, floors, fixtures, and caulking.

One highly important bathroom maintenance item is caulking. Why is that so important? Here's six reasons why:

1. Bad caulking around tubs allows water to seep down the wall to the floor and damage both.
2. A shower pan-to-wall caulking failure can allow water to seep under the pan and cause floor rot and mold growth.
3. Caulking around sinks keeps water from damaging the counter, wall, and flooring.
4. Depending on the floor, caulking can prevent water from seeping down along the edges to the subfloor.
5. Water can leak through damaged caulking and cause damage to cabinets or flooring. You'll notice that all these reasons for caulking have one thing in common: keeping water from getting to the subfloor and costing you a lot of money.
6. Bad caulking makes a home look like a dump. If you're selling, it can make the difference between sale or no sale, full price or low offer.

All About Bathroom Caulking

Check out the caulking section of any home improvement center and you'll be amazed at the many different caulks. The different formulations are designed for different applications. Latex caulk, for example, is designed for interior sealing and can be painted to match.

HOW-TO-CAULK WEBSITES

www.naturalhandyman.com/iip/infxtra/infcau.shtm
www.repair-home.com/how_to/caulk.htm
www.bathtubdoctor.com/services/caulk.php
www.ehow.com/how_114916_seal-wall-joints.html

Table 4-2 gives you a broad overview of the different types and their applications:

Most manufacturers put a lot of info on their tubes, so read the labels before you buy. For bathroom tubs and showers, pick a product that is designed for the type of surface you have. Many professionals use silicone caulk, and it does a good job, but the downside is you can't clean up spills or get it off your hands. Unless you're a professional with caulking skills, it's better to

Table 4-2. Caulk types and their uses.

Type	Use	Adhesion	Durability	Pros	Cons
Latex	Interior wood	Porous	Fair	Paintable, water cleanup, fast curing.	Don't use for wet environments.
Acrylic Latex	Interior and exterior	Porous or wood	Good	Paintable, water cleanup, UV resistant.	Not for wet areas.
Silicone	Nonporous	Good	Long-lasting	Flexible, doesn't shrink.	Can't paint it. Doesn't adhere to porous surfaces, solvent cleanup.
Acrylic Latex/ Silicone	All purpose interior and exterior	Good	Long-lasting	Paintable, water cleanup.	Not as good on nonporous surfaces.
Polyurethane	All purpose	Good	Long-lasting	Paintable, seals gaps well, low shrinkage.	Harder to use, solvent cleanup.
Butyl Rubber	Exterior only	Good	Good	Paintable, good for temperature extremes.	Hard to apply, solvent cleanup. Don't use inside.

go with Polyseamseal Tub and Tile Caulk or similar latex, mildew-proof products. They work great and clean up with soap and water.

However, if your tub is fiberglass with ceramic tile walls or fiberglass sections with caulked joints, silicone is recommended.

To recaulk the seams in your bathroom, follow these six easy steps:

1. Patching caulked areas doesn't work too well, so it's better to remove all the caulk and redo the entire tub or shower. Remove all the old caulk, clean the area thoroughly, and then vacuum. Any loose material or dust can compromise your joint.

2. Degrease and clean the joint with alcohol, but if there's mildew present treat the joints with a fungicide and then thoroughly dry.

3. Use a hair dryer or small heater to dry the joint completely before caulking or it may not stick. You can also use a hair dryer to soften old caulking and make it easier to remove.

4. If you have only one or two bathrooms you may want to buy 5.5 oz.

plastic tubes of caulking instead of a caulking gun and cartridges. There's less waste, and beginners often find tubes easier to work with.

5.   Cut the tip of the cartridge or tube at a 45-degree angle and start at the far end of the joint and work toward you. Squeeze out a uniform bead of caulk into the joint as you move the tip along the joint. When you get to end, put your finger over the tip or insert a nail to stop the caulk from flowing.

6.   The next step is to tool the joint, and the best way to do that is with your finger. That can get messy, so you'll want to get a package of latex gloves—the kind your dentist, doctor, and car mechanic use—especially if you use silicone caulk. You can also use a putty knife with a rounded end, plastic spoon, wood tongue depressor, or butter knife. Go over the joint only once, don't dab at it but run your finger (dipping your gloved finger in water helps) along the joint, forcing the caulk into the gap. You want to create a smooth wedge of caulk over the joint. Yes, it's art work: The more you do it the better you get—just like painting. If you mess up a joint, clean it out and do it over; no big deal. Let the caulk cure for about 24 hours and clean up with a razor blade.

Areas in your bathroom that are especially important and you should inspect every couple of months are:

- Around bathtubs and floor-to-shower seams.
- Around sinks and where the vanity top meets the wall.
- Around the base of the tub or shower enclosure where it meets the floor.
- Along the baseboard to floor seam.
- Anywhere water could get through to the subfloor.
- Do not caulk around where the toilet bowl meets the floor. If the wax seal fails (see Chapter 2), you want to know about it fast so it doesn't damage the subfloor.

Although caulking can prevent water from seeping where it not supposed to, additional strategies are needed to keep bathroom mold under control—such as frequently checking under sinks, installing good venting systems that exhaust moist air to the outside, and installing watertight shower enclosures. Homebuyers tend to get uptight when they or their inspectors find bathroom mold.

Bath Remodeling: What Pays, What Doesn't

There are two ways to measure the return on bathroom improvements or any home improvement for that matter:

1.   If you don't do the upgrades, what will it cost you in lower offers and more days on the market. Home sellers usually lose more money this way than from too much improvement.

2.   The second measurement is more direct. Suppose you spend $7,000 to remodel your bath. Will it increase the value of your home by the same amount? Looking at national statistics can be misleading because real estate values vary from neighborhood to neighborhood. The best way is to have a friendly Realtor run a list of what similar homes to yours have sold for with and without the improvements. Local appraisers also have a good feel for what improvements have good payback for your area.

Typically, the following bathroom improvements will more than pay for themselves:

- Replacing a beat up vanity with a pedestal sink or new vanity, counter-top, and sink.
- Replacing vinyl flooring with tile especially if you do the install.
- New tub or shower surround if it's consistent with your price range. In-other-words, tearing out your tub-shower combo and replacing it with a double-size imported marble shower-steam room wouldn't have a good payback. You want to keep upgrades consistent with what other homes in your price range have.
- An attractive light bar above sink. Good bathroom lighting is a must.
- If it's an older home, updating wiring and outlets with a GFI outlet.
- An attractive paint scheme that ties the bathroom into the rest of the home.

In addition to upgrading baths, adding a new bathroom is often a good investment that adds more to the value of your home than the cost. This is especially true if you have an older home with one bath and everyone else on your block has two baths.

Adding a bath when you finish off a basement, attic or part of the master bedroom is usually a good investment. Again, before spending big bucks, make sure the neighborhood will support the investment.

BATHROOM REMODELING WEBSITES

www.remodeling.hw.net/content/CvsV/CostvsValue.asp?articleID = 211765&
    sectionID = 173

www.hgtvpro.com/hpro/di_bathrooms/article/
   0,2618,HPRO_20173_3727707,00.html
www.design.hgtv.com/bath/sub_topic_03.aspx?t = 2&st = 8

In addition to bathrooms, kitchens are at the top of the list of what buyers zero in on first. If these two meet their expectations, the home goes on their short list. Even if you're not planning on selling in the near future, these rooms are what family and friends see most. Kitchens are where everyone wants to be: that's where the action, the refrigerator, and the food are. It's no wonder then that kitchens are the most remodeled, upgraded, fretted over, and decorated areas in the home, and the most covered in TV shows and magazines.

The next section will cover kitchens and how to make them look their best along with how to save some serious bucks.

HOW TO MAKE YOUR KITCHEN LOOK ITS BEST

Like bathrooms, how much of your remodeling dollar increases the value of your home depends on the area you live. That means you'll want to do some homework before writing checks at the nearest home center.

First step is go through homes for sale and open houses in your area to see what upgrades your neighborhood will support. For instance, are homeowners upgrading counters to Corian™, granite, concrete, laminate, or whatever is fashionable? How about cabinets, what's the current rage: oak, stressed aspen, or dark cherry?

A good way to find out what's current is go through builder's open houses. They spend a lot of money and time making their model homes appealing to the largest number of people.

Builder's decorators strive to create shock and awe with color and furnishings, so that when you walk back into your own home you're dissatisfied with your humble dwelling and start crunching numbers.

But what's exciting is that you can take ideas not only from open houses but from magazines, TV shows, and homes for sale—to personalize your home while adding to its value.

A good place to start making your kitchen look its best is the floors. As previously discussed, tile and wood laminates wear and look good. If you do the work yourself, you get a lot more bang for the buck. Most home improvements you can make yourself, and developing new skills will give you a lot of satisfaction.

MONEY-SAVING TIP

If you can hold a pencil and draw a reasonably straight line you can do a great tile job. Many home centers have free classes and rent the tile cutters and tools. Tiling your kitchen, bath, and entryway floors make your home look great, and it's the best way to add value without a lot of cost.

After floors, cabinets are key features of a kitchen, and there are a lot of options for making drab cabinets attractive. In fact, one home renovator with a twenty-year track record says she has never yet replaced kitchen cabinets on any of their rehabs. They've been able to refinish and rebuild cabinets so they're attractive. It must work because the homes they renovate sell quickly and for top price.

WEBSITES FOR MORE REFINISHING HOW-TO

www.finefurniturefinishing.com/newsletter10.html
www.inin.essortment.com/cabinetrefinish_rgqc.htm
www.lowes.com/lowes/lkn?action = howTo&tp = HomeDecor/CabFceLft.html#4
www.thisoldhouse.com/toh/knowhow/kitchen/article/0,16417,202424,00.html
www.doityourself.com/stry/kitchencabinets

Here are some alternatives to laying out big money for all new kitchen cabinets: (this also applies to sinks):

- If there are not enough cabinets in your kitchen and you can't find additional matching ones, you can still keep the old cabinet frames. Replace the doors and hardware on the old cabinets to match the new ones; refinish both old and new to match. However, because the old and new wood frames may not match, painting both a gloss white or other light color is often the best way to go.
- Strip the cabinet's finish, sand, and refinish with new hardware. For example, if you have 1980s dark wood cabinets, you should be able to strip the finish, sand, and stain a lighter color. With new hardware, you wouldn't know it was the same cabinets. If the finish won't come off, you can always paint the wood a light gloss color.
- It's amazing how many complete sets of cabinets are discarded by re-modelers. Many of these are in excellent condition or can be refin-

ished. Check the yellow pages for salvage yards and second-hand outlets.

Check with cabinet shops for seconds, unfinished units, and cancelled orders.

- Look for discontinued lines and sales at home centers. It's amazing the deals you can get if you shop around.
- Sometimes a good cleaning, finish coat and new hardware can make your cabinets look new. Also consider adding molding on the doors to create a custom look.
- There are also companies who can glue a thin wood veneer or plastic laminate to cabinets that creates a new look for less than replacing them.

KITCHEN DECORATING TIP

Give your kitchen personality by varying the height and depth of the cabinets. For example, create a staggered line or put a taller cabinet over the stove. Glass doors on one or two units break up a monotonous line of identical doors. Adding crown molding and cabinet-to-wall trim also works well.

If you would rather start over and buy new cabinets, there are a lot of exciting options to choose from. Basically, there are three ways you can go:

1. *Stock cabinets* are those you find at home centers ready for delivery. It's usually what-you-see-is-what-you-get. Typically you'll pay $50 to $200 per linear foot.
2. Buying *semi-custom cabinets* is like buying a car: Take the base model and add what accessories you want from the options list. Cost typically runs from $200 to $600 per cabinet foot.
3. *Custom cabinets* are made specially for your kitchen layout with the latest cutting edge design and options. Custom cabinet shops usually charge from about $500 per foot on up to what a Ferrari costs.

The following shopping tips can help you keep costs in suborbit:

- Consider going with oak or white laminate cabinets. These are less expensive than cherry, pine, or exotic woods.
- Go with better cabinets and cut costs elsewhere, such as countertops and appliances; replacing those later on could help stretch the budget.

- Consider going granite on an island and laminate on all the other counters.
- Choose veneered doors instead of solid wood.
- Keep existing appliances and refinish to match your new color décor.

Along with cabinets, countertops are a kitchen's focal point and help define the personality of a kitchen. There are lots of countertop options, each with its pros and cons. It boils down to how much abuse the counter is going to get and what surface you really like.

To get the most functionality and economy plus create a dramatic effect, don't overlook mixing styles and materials. For example, the island top could be granite, marble, wood or whatever works best for your lifestyle. If you're a dynamite pastry chef, the island could be marble and the counters another material, such as stainless steel or laminate. You can be as creative as you like: no more straight line of cabinets and a boring length of laminate counter from the kitchen dark ages.

Most popular countertop options are shown in Table 4-3.

An important touch to an impressive kitchen is lighting. As in countertops and flooring, there are a lot of options. If you have recessed lighting, new broad spectrum bulbs that approximate natural daylight can make a big difference.

For replacing light fixtures, consider a low-voltage cable-and-rail system. The rails are attached to the ceiling and can be bent into shapes. Two parallel cables are typically stretched from wall to wall, and light fixtures are attached to the wires. They can be moved anywhere along the cable.

In practice, you can have a couple of lights drop down over a island, dining table of other areas that need lighting. You may want to check out lighting supply stores that have working displays and help you tailor a system to fit your home.

MORE INFORMATION ON TRACK AND CABLE-AND-RAIL SYSTEMS

www.signonsandiego.com/uniontrib/20061022/news_1hs22ceiling.html

www.lightwavesconcept.com/home.php?cat = 251&tcm_re = Menu-_-LightRail-_-Systems

www.con-techlighting.com/catalogs/OdysseyLineVoltageRail.pd

Also pay special attention to the cutting-edge lighting in new-home open houses and home decorating magazines. Lighting is an inexpensive way (typically under $500) to add high tech to your kitchen.

Table 4-3. Countertop materials: pros and cons.

Option	Pros	Cons	Cost
Wood	Can be sanded and refinished, warm custom look.	Needs lots of care, can burn, and water leaves stains.	About $100 per sq. ft. installed, depending on wood.
Granite	Popular, beautiful, durable, and heat resistant.	Very porous and needs a penetrating sealer every few months to prevent stains.	$50 to $100 plus per sq.ft. installed.
Soapstone and slate	Softer than granite but less porous and doesn't need sealing. Rustic look.	Scratches and chips easily.	$50 to $100 plus per sq.ft. installed.
Marble	Warm and soft looking, but not too practical for all the counters. Serious bakers may want to add a marble section or do an island top.	Stains easily from food acids.	$50 to $100 plus per sq.ft. installed.
Pyrolave™	Glazed lava with colored enamel added, hard, durable comes in all colors.	May be difficult to find, hard on glasses.	$75 to $100 per sq.ft. installed.
Concrete	Beautiful with endless color and design possibilities. Heat resistant and durable.	After sealing, needs waxing to maintain stain resistance.	$75 to $100 sq.ft. installed.
Engineered Stone: Silestone, Cambria, Zodiaq, etc.	Heat resistant, durable, easy to maintain, lots of patterns and color choices.	Not as natural looking as granite or other natural stone.	$50 to $100 per sq.ft. installed.
Ceramic Tile	Heat resistant, unlimited styles, sizes and colors. Easy do-it-yourself install.	Grout needs occasionally cleaning and sealing.	$15 to $75 a sq. ft. installed.
Laminates	Wide range of styles, colors, and edge treatments. Very economical and attractive.	Easy to burn, scratch, or damage.	$5 to $25 a sq.ft. installed.

(continues)

Table 4-3. Continued.

Option	Pros	Cons	Cost
Solid Surfaces, Corian™	Can take a lot of abuse, easy to clean, don't stain, can be sanded, lots of colors and styles.	Not heat resistant, looks less natural than stone.	$50 to $100 per sq.ft. installed.
Laminates	Unlimited styles and colors, can be jazzed up with a variety of edge treatments.	Not heat or scratch resistant.	$5 to $25 sq.ft. installed.
Metal: stainless, copper, zinc.	Heat proof, does not react to acids and stains.	Can scratch. Copper and zinc dull with age.	$75 to $125 sq.ft. installed.

Of course, no kitchen can look better than its appliances, and sometimes it's a challenge trying to decide whether to keep or replace them. Typical life expectancy for kitchen appliances is:

Electric Range	17 years
Gas Range	19 years
Refrigerator	14 to 17 years
Microwave	11 years
Garbage Disposal	10 years
Dishwasher	10 years

Some appliances may last a lot longer, while others die the day after the warranty expires. In reality, there are several ways you can go when deciding on what to upgrade and what not to upgrade:

1. If the color or finish of the appliance isn't a problem, keep it and spend the funds on other upgrades; possibly replace it later on.
2. When the new kitchen remodel changed colors so that the appliances no longer fit the décor, you can save quite a few bucks by having a professional paint the appliances.
3. Bite the bullet and replace the appliances now. If your appliances are at or over the age range listed above, there's an additional consideration: energy efficiency. New appliances consume less power than older models.

ENERGY-SAVING TIP

When shopping for appliances, look for the EPA's ENERGY STAR label. Appliances with that label use up to 30 percent less power than those sold as recently as 2001. That means you can help out the environment and save money too, often enough to justify replacing older appliances.

With kitchen and baths looking good, the next area to consider is living and family rooms.

LIVING AND FAMILY ROOMS THAT ADD VALUE

Living rooms have taken a back burner position the last few years, with emphasis more on family and great rooms. In new homes, living room size has often shrunk to where it's almost an afterthought. Still, they're important because visitors will pass through or by the living room on the way to the kitchen, and you want to create a favorable impression. This is especially important if you have an older home where the entryway opens into the living room.

Some living-room decorating suggestions are:

• Of course, a dynamite paint job goes a long way to making the room impressive. This is also a room you can be more expressive with. For example, one homeowner painted three walls a light beige and the wall facing the entry door a dark red. She then included that color in the furniture, accessories, and trim for an impressive effect. The owners could also have carried the dark red color throughout the house to tie the décor together.

• If the entryway door opens into the living room, you can tile or install wood flooring in a half circle or square in front of the door. This creates an attractive entryway. A light decorative screen can block the view into the kitchen or rest of the living room.

• Window treatments are an important part of a room's décor. Small rooms should avoid heavy drapes; go with light colored blinds or shutters instead. The more light a room gets the better it looks.

• Carpets, rugs, and furniture should be on the light side.

• Scale is also critical. In a smaller room, less is often more. Avoid oversize furniture, large pictures, over-grown plants, and anything that overwhelms the room. The super-sized sectional sofas, armchairs, and coffee tables look better in a larger family room.

Family rooms or great rooms have taken center stage from living rooms the past few years because they are close to or part of the kitchen, where the action (food) is. Many family rooms also have vaulted or cathedral ceilings that open many exciting decorating possibilities.

In fact, so important are family rooms that, according to *Remodeling* magazine's annual "Cost vs. Value Report" for 2006, family room additions returned 113.3 percent, or $63,556, on an average cost of $56,111 to build.

Does this mean you can bump out a wall, tack a family room onto your kitchen, and get more than the cost back when you sell? Not always. Remember, real estate is local, so before you draw up plans, check out what other homes similar to yours have done in the area. Look at what homes have sold for that have added family rooms versus homes that haven't. Some areas can support all sorts of home improvements while other neighborhoods just a few blocks away can't.

Other less costly family-room options are finishing off a basement or attic. Here, too, you'll need to look at recent sales in the area to determine the payback. If you do add a family room, consider adding a bath at the same time: It's cheaper to add one when construction is underway than later. Also, another bath may add enough value to your home to justify the cost.

As for decorating family rooms, it's more relaxed. However, if the family room connects to the kitchen, coordinating the colors and trim adds to the flow.

DON'T FORGET BEDROOMS AND LAUNDRY ROOMS

Unlike family rooms, visitors don't often see the bedrooms, and decorating them often takes a back seat. But there are some things you can and should do enhance your home's value:

- If possible use the same floor covering in all bedrooms. A common color or decorating theme ties all the rooms together.

- Closets are a big item with some people. If you have walk-in closets, organize them and make sure they're well lighted. Older homes with small closets will need more creativity. Decluttering and adding organizers are a good start. Also, painting them a bright or gloss white makes them appear larger. Adding lighting can also help.

- A bedroom light/fan combo can add a decorator touch. Match the fan size to the bedroom. For example, a large bedroom with vaulted ceilings can accommodate a large fan where a small bedroom would need a scaled-down model.

• Window treatments should also fit the room. Blinds and shutters make a room look larger than heavy drapes will.

• Some homeowners like to decorate the master bedroom with creative colors and patterned wall coverings. However, when you decide to sell, it's better to restore the décor back to vanilla neutral.

INTERESTING BEDROOM-DECORATING WEBSITES

www.interiordec.about.com/od/bedroomdecor
www.creativehomemaking.com/home_decorating/bedrooms.shtml
www.home.ivillage.com/decorating/bedrooms/0,,8sgq,00.html
www.homeandfamilynetwork.com/Decorating.html
www.decorate-redecorate.com/decorate-bedroom.html
www.realsimple.com/realsimple/package/0,21861,1013123,00.html

For many homeowners the laundry room is further down the upgrade list than the bedrooms. But in reality, the laundry room has come up the food chain of importance the last few years. To see how far, check out the laundry rooms in new home construction. Some rival small bedrooms in size.

LAUNDRY ROOM WEBSITES

www.interiordec.about.com/od/laundryroom1/
www.servicemagic.com/article.show.7-Essential-Laundry-Room-
    Solutions.8288.html
www.ehow.com/how_10820_jazz-laundry-room.html

If your laundry is in the basement, you probably have the space to enclose and make it an impressive room without paying a lot. Also, some basements have plumbing stubbed in for a bath, which can be used to create a half or three-quarter (with shower) bath/laundry room combo. This is an economical way to add a bath to your home's stats.

As covered in previous sections, developing tiling skills can pay big dividends. If you're looking for a place to start, this is it. A downstairs bath/laundry combo is just the right size for a first project.

*   *   *

The five biggest mistakes homeowners make when trying to improve their homes' interiors are listed in Table 4-4.

You could spend a lifetime upgrading and improving your home's interior. But to maintain value and keep your home looking its best you need to spend time on the exterior as well: it's what keeps the rain off your head. How to do that is detailed in Chapter 5.

Table 4-4. The biggest interior-improvement mistakes homeowners make.

Mistake	Suggested Action
Keeping old inefficient appliances and fixtures	Keeping old appliances is often not cost- or energy-wise. Replace with EPA's ENERGY STAR-rated appliances for maximum savings.
Not keeping the interior in good condition	It's cheaper to fix or upgrade items along the way. If you decide to sell, you won't have a huge get-ready-to-sell bill.
Not coordinating the home's décor	To make a home stand out, the colors and décor should flow from room to room. Pick a theme or accent color and carry it throughout the home.
Adding a room or addition that overvalues the home	Adding on to a home is a good idea if the neighborhood will support it. Have other homes in your area added on? If you do, will you get your investment back?
Not decorating to the home's style	Make sure improvements like door styles or cabinet styles go with your home's style. For example, you wouldn't want contemporary appliances in a Craftsman-style home.

CHAPTER 5

EXTERIOR MAINTENANCE AND IMPROVEMENTS THAT ADD VALUE

Maintaining and improving your home's exterior is especially important, because much of a home's value and pride of ownership comes from curb appeal. It's usually not expensive or difficult, but it does entail staying on top of potential problems to keep the home weather-tight.

Once a home's exterior components are compromised by damage or neglect, or are just worn out, water starts doing its thing. When that happens, the dollar-calibrated repair meter spins faster than a cabbie's mileage meter. It's much cheaper to head off problems before you feel raindrops falling on your head during dinner.

Unfortunately, too many homeowners wait until they want to sell before thinking about exterior maintenance, and in the rush it often doesn't get done. This is reflected by telling comments in their ads and MLS remarks, such as:

"Must see the inside . . ."

"Bigger than it looks . . ."

"Just needs a little TLC . . ."

"Roofing allowance . . ."

And so on, but you get the idea. Owners and agents hope to minimize the problems when in reality they are throwing away thousands of dollars needlessly. Buyers aren't dummies, and their pencils are sharp.

But there is good news in all this: If you can turn a screwdriver and tell your right hand from your left, you can do most of the repairs needed to keep your home's exterior in good condition. And as a bonus, you can improve and increase its value significantly.

Some of the critical items covered in this chapter are:

✓ How to make sure your home's outside components are watertight
✓ How to upgrade your home's curb appeal
✓ How to keep gutters draining
✓ Wells and septic systems
✓ How to keep concrete and asphalt looking good

PREVENTING WATER DAMAGE

Whenever you talk about a home's exterior you're really discussing the weather and how to keep it from getting into the home. A critical first line of defense against water infiltrating the home or causing exterior damage is the gutter or roof drainage system.

Some homes don't have gutters and rely on the roof extending beyond the wall to divert water a couple of feet out from the foundation, but this creates serious problems. If the ground doesn't have enough slope to drain water away from the foundation, water can damage it and can seep into the crawl space or basement.

Also, water spilling over the eaves can kick up mud onto the siding, which leaves an ugly stain that's not easy to remove. These stains and possible siding damage can lower your curb appeal and your home's value considerably. It's a red flag that tells all who see this home that it's not well taken care of.

Rain Gutter Savvy

The first step in weatherproofing your home is install a gutter system or make sure the existing one is in good shape and is handling the runoff. If your home needs a new system, Table 5-1 lists some common options.

Table 5-1. Common rain-gutter options

Type	Pros	Cons	Cost $
Vinyl	Can be installed by homeowner, maintains color, dent resistant, won't rust.	Easy to damage in cold climates and gets brittle as it ages.	$3 to $5 per foot installed.
Aluminum	Color weathers well, can be installed seamless, good for cold climates.	Prone to denting.	$4 to $8 per foot installed.
Copper, Stainless	Long-lasting, copper develops an attractive patina.	Very expensive, can dent, needs professional install.	$15 to $20 per foot installed.
Sectional Gutters	User install, can be aluminum or vinyl.	Seams can leak.	Least expensive install.
Seamless Gutters (best choice)	No seams to leak, easy maintenance.	Need professional install.	$5 to $8 per foot installed.

A new vinyl or aluminum gutter system for a typical 2,500 sq. ft. home would cost approximately $700 to $1,200 installed. In addition, you would want to add inexpensive extensions to the down spouts to route water at least six feet from the foundation. The costs involved here are much less than replacing siding or repairing interior damage from rain water entering through a window well. Figure 5-1 shows how a slip-on extension can route water safely onto the lawn and away from foundations and window wells. For more a permanent low profile, the extension in Figure 5-2 runs underground.

HELPFUL RAIN-GUTTER WEBSITES

www.doityourself.com/stry/vinylraingutters
www.hometips.com/hyhw/shell/128gut.html
www.thisoldhouse.com/toh/knowhow/repair/article/0,16417,487931,00.html

If you have a gutter system already installed, inspect it twice a year (fall and spring) to make sure it's working. Use the maintenance checklist in Table 5-2.

Yes, cleaning out gutters twice a year is a pain, but beware of gutter-

Figure 5-1.

cleaning silver bullets that promise to eliminate it. "There ain't no shortcuts, unfortunately," according to this author / homeowner / gutter cleaner who lives in the middle of a grove of deciduous trees and is still looking for a quick and easy solution. However, there are homeowners who have had good results with the "Waterfall"-type gutter guards, and they may be worth checking out for your area.

Once your gutter system is fine-tuned and able to divert roof run-off away from the house, it's important to take a quick look at the landscaping. Does the landscaping divert water away from the home? If it does, you're in good shape. But if it doesn't, you'll need to move some dirt around until it does.

MONEY-SAVING TIP

Many homeowners find out too late that run-off water from outside the home is not covered by homeowners insurance. For this kind of coverage you'll need additional Federal flood insurance available through most insurance companies.

Table 5-2. Gutter maintenance checklist.

Job	Action needed
Clean out the muck.	Remove any screens or debris guards and clean out the sludge with a plastic scoop.
Remove the elbows.	Use a drill to remove the elbow fasteners. If they're attached with rivets, use a ¹/₈-inch bit to drill them out. Clean out the goop.
Scrub the gutters.	Using a stiff brush clean out the gutters and elbows and flush with water.
Replace elbows.	Reattach the elbows with ³/₈-inch hex-head metal screws (zip screws). Replacing the rivets with hex-heads makes the twice-yearly cleaning much easier.
Check straps.	Downspouts have metal straps at each end. If they're loose, re-attach or replace if needed.
Channel the water.	Put 4-foot to 5-foot extensions on the downspouts to channel water away from the foundation and window wells (see Figure 5-1).
Fix sagging gutters.	Probably a nail has come loose letting that section sag. Use a hammer and pry bar to remove the nails and clips. Replace the nails and clips or hangers. Spacing should be about 24 inches. Roof-mounted gutters are fixed by replacing the straps anchored to the roof with roofing nails.
Prevent water from damaging fascia.	Slide a length of aluminum drip edge (available at home centers) under the roofing or shingles and over the gutter's back edge. Lift the shingles and nail the drip edge to roof deck (not the shingles) with roofing nails every 24 inches.
Recaulk leaking seams.	Use a heat gun to make sure the surface is perfectly dry. Apply a generous amount of aluminum joint sealer or butyl caulking evenly over the seam. Use latex gloves; these sealants are hard to get off hands.

If you've just bought the home, it's a good idea during the next hard rain to walk around the yard with an umbrella and observe where the water is going and how well your gutter system is working.

The next line of defense against the elements is the home's siding. Its job is to keep water in liquid and vapor form outside with the bugs and spiders.

MAINTAINING AND REPLACING SIDING

Wood siding is commonly used in older frame homes and some newer ones. Typically it can last hundreds of years if it's maintained properly. But it's the word "maintained" that's critical here: Wood siding has to be painted and caulked every few years, or water, mold, and insect infestation will quickly destroy it.

Figure 5-2.

It's far cheaper to maintain the siding than getting an equity loan to replace it, or get stuck having to reduce your price when a home inspector finds serious problems. Use the following checklist every spring and fall to keep your siding in top shape:

• Look for signs of paint failure, such as blistering, peeling, and worn areas. The question you should continually ask yourself is: "Can water get through here?" A caulking gun, sandpaper, and paint brush are your best friends to keep the weather and critters at bay.

• Also look for mold, mildew, and blackening on the paint. If you find any of these, remove them immediately with a fungicide or bleach solution. Make a note to use a paint with a fungicide next time you recoat.

• To correct paint failure in only one or two areas, scrape and sand the bad area and apply a matching coat of quality, fungus-resistant paint.

• Carefully inspect where pipes and wiring enter the house and reseal with a good exterior caulk or canned foam insulation. Also look at where the siding butts up to chimneys, inside corners, and any other dissimilar surfaces. Scrape out old caulking and reapply to gaps or cracks that are not watertight.

• Checked and peeling paint are signs of water vapor getting behind the painted surface. Look for sources of infiltration: poor caulking, cracks, seams, and joints.

Cedar Siding

Cedar siding comes in several different applications, with tongue-and-groove, beveled, vertical shiplap, shingle, or shake being the most common. Some homeowners prefer to use a semi-transparent stain to protect and keep the wood looking new; some use a pigment stain while others let the wood weather to a natural silver gray.

INTERESTING INFORMATION ABOUT SIDING

www.wrcla.org/specifications_and_publications/default.htm
www.askthebuilder.com/
    066_Bleeding_Redwood_And_Cedar_Siding_Stains.shtml
www.siding4u.com/vinyl-siding-cost-calculator.php

Although the natural grey is attractive, letting cedar weather without any treatment doesn't always work out. Mold can gain a foothold and stain the surface with dark splotches. If not treated with a fungicide or chlorine solution, mold can ruin the siding.

Upkeep on cedar siding entails replacing split boards, keeping mold at bay, sealing empty knotholes, and replacing rusting nails or screws with stainless steel or other nonrusting fasteners.

Vinyl/Aluminum Siding

Vinyl/aluminum siding is popular because it's economical, has a long lifespan, maintains its color, and doesn't require painting every few years. It's a good choice for homeowners who are tired of painting or staining wood siding because it can often be installed over the existing siding.

Maintenance is a strong point because when grime starts to build up, power washing is all you have to do to keep it looking good.

Fiber-Cement Siding

Fiber-cement siding is another good choice for new or replacement siding. Made out of cement, cellulose fibers, and other additives, it's a stable, durable, and economical option. You can paint it any color or it can be ordered pre-painted. Even better, it's available in styles that resemble stucco, wood clapboards, or even cedar shingles, and it's highly fire-resistant.

With fiber-cement siding, about the only maintenance required is to re-paint it every ten years or so.

Stucco Siding

Stucco siding is a mix of Portland cement, sand, and other fibers. It's durable, economical, comes in a large array of colors and patterns, and can also be painted.

Unfortunately, one type of synthetic stucco, known as EIFS (Exterior Insu-lation and Finish Systems), has been associated with moisture problems. The underlying wood on EIFS-sided homes may suffer rot damage. However, other types of synthetic stucco are quite durable. Still, it's wise to hire a professional to inspect the home if you're not sure what type you have. Early detection of water seepage can save big bucks later on.

Table 5-3 compares the most common options for replacing siding:

Because there are so many siding options, it's important to ask lots of questions about the product and the installing contractor, so you can compare bids accurately. Also, it's critical to use a reputable contractor experienced in the specific siding you're installing. (Chapter 6 details how to find and work with siding contractors.) The manufacturer's warranty can be voided if the product isn't installed properly. In addition, don't forget to factor in other costs, such as tearing off old siding, adding insulation wrap, and replacing any damaged wood.

Also important is removing any shrubs, trees, and vines that are growing against the home. Create at least a two-foot space between siding and plant growth; this will help control mildew and rot, and avoid damage from branches rubbing against the siding.

If you have wood siding or trim, you need to protect it by painting or staining every few years; it's part of homeownership. The next section shows how to protect your investment.

EXTERIOR PAINTING TIPS

Basically, there are two ways to coat exterior wood: stain or paint. Both are formulated with pigments for color, and a water or oil base with binders and hardening agents. Stains have less pigment and resin than paints, which makes them a better choice if you want to retain more of the wood color and texture.

The biggest difference is in how stain and paint react with the wood sur-face. Stains penetrate raw wood like warm mustard spilled on your favorite

Table 5-3. Siding comparisons.

Siding Type	Pros	Cons	Approximate Cost
Vinyl	Economical. Water-, insect-, mold-, and fade-resistant. Easy to install over old siding.	Dents, brittle in cold weather, environmental concerns.	$2 to $3 per sq. ft. installed
Aluminum	Similar to vinyl, more insulation factor. Lots of color choices.	Not a good choice if you live near a golf course. More expensive than vinyl. Dents easily.	$3 to $5 per sq. ft. installed.
Fiber Cement	Durable, lots of colors and patterns, resistant to about everything. Economical.	Heavier than aluminum and vinyl.	$3 to $4 per sq. ft. installed.
Wood Siding: Cedar	Attractive, long-lasting if maintained, weather-resistant.	Needs more maintenance, not very mold- or fire-resistant.	$4 to $7 per sq. ft. installed.
Wood Siding: Paint Grade	Same as cedar.	Needs painting every few years.	$3 to $5 per sq. ft. installed.
Stucco: Sand and Cement	Resistant to weather, long-lasting, lots of color and style choices, fire- and rot-resistant.	Needs professional installation. On re-siding, old siding needs a tear-off, adding to costs.	$3 to $6 per sq. ft. installed.
Stucco: Latex	Same as above.	Needs professional install. More expensive than sand/cement stucco.	$6 to $9 per sq. ft. installed.
Brick	Attractive and durable, what other sidings are compared to.	Very expensive and usually not practicable for re-siding.	$8 to $15 per sq. ft. installed.
Faux Stone	Attractive, durable, and great for trim.	Expensive, often used with other less expensive sidings to cut costs.	$10 to $15 per sq. ft. installed.
Natural Stone	Same as above.	Same as above.	Up to $30 per sq. ft. installed.

shirt or blouse. Paint, on the other hand, bonds to wood surfaces and creates a thin film with little penetration into the wood fibers.

Advantages of stains on previously stained or unpainted wood are:

- Moisture trapped behind stain coatings usually bleeds through and evaporates on the surface. With paint, water cannot bleed through, so blistering and peeling result.
- Surface prep is easier. All you have to do is clean off dirt and mildew and re-stain.
- Stains are available with UV blockers, fungicides, and wood preservatives.
- You can get stains in semitransparent and solid colors to match the effect you want and the surface to be treated.

The bottom line is: If you have cedar, redwood, or other wood siding that is new or previously stained, you're probably better off staying with stain. But if you have siding that has been previously painted, you need to stick to paint, preferably acrylic latex or similar high quality products.

Although exterior house paint has a flat, nonreflective finish that tends to hide minor imperfections, you still have to prep the surface for good results.

HOUSE PAINTING HOW-TO WEBSITES

www.easy2diy.com/cm/easy/diy_ht_index.asp?page_id=35720475
www.architecture.about.com/od/paint/paint_your_house_tips_for_
    choosing_exterior_colors.htm
www.servicemagic.com/article.show.exterior-painting-techniques.8598.html
www.doityourself.com/scat/decoratingexterior

Also, color choices are endless, and for some homeowners that creates a problem. Paint choices made from color chips at the paint store won't look the same on your house. It's best to paint a test section first. Brush a wide swath on the back of the house first and see what it looks like in the real world, especially if you're changing colors. The pale blue color on a paint chip can look nearly bright blue when applied. You've undoubtedly driven by homes and wondered what the owners were thinking when they picked out their house colors.

One couple, for example, who wanted their home painted went to a local hardware store and picked out what appeared to be pale yellow from the paint chip display. They bought the paint, stacked the gallon cans on their porch, hired a handyman-painter and left for a ten-day vacation. When they returned, they were shocked to find their home's new color was closer to a mid-yellow. The neighbors called it the mustard house and before the owners could arrange for a repaint, the weather turned wet and cold for a few weeks. The home did get repainted, but the owners had to live with a color they didn't like for about six weeks, not to mention paying the costs of the new paint and a professional painter.

Lessons learned are to test the color before you order it in gallons, and to stay involved if you hire a painter, so you know the job is done the way you want.

However, before you paint, the critical first step is surface prep. Skipping this step is like forgetting to add eggs to the cake mix; you won't like the result. Use the following steps to guide you through surface prep:

1. Examine every square foot of your home's exterior and look for mildew, peeling, or checked paint. Remove mildew with a solution of one part bleach to two parts water.
2. If the paint is peeling, it's likely that water is getting under it and causing the problem; correct this before painting. Likely sources are failed caulking, bad insulation letting moist interior air seep through, or leaking flashing or gutters. For an older home, you may have to add insulation and a vapor barrier. Otherwise look for areas that water could get into and have your caulking gun at the ready.
3. For seriously deteriorated paint, you can sometimes clean most of it off the siding with a pressure washer. However, you'll need to keep the pressure under 2,000 psi (pounds per square inch) and the spray head about a foot away from the surface to avoid damaging the siding.
4. Depending on how bad the siding surface is, you may have to sand it. Palm and orbital sanders work well with medium grit (#100) sandpaper. The goal is to remove any loose paint and feather the patches of old paint into a smooth surface.
5. Make sure the siding surface is thoroughly dry before painting.

After you've completed the prep work, the semi-final step is to apply a coat of primer. Many homeowners skip this part, but if you want all your grunt work to last as long as possible, go with a primer coat. It's best to get the primer and top coat from the same manufacturer so you have complete compatibility.

The primer and final coat can be applied with a 4-inch synthetic bristle brush or a 6-inch or 9-inch roller. Some homeowners use an airless spray gun, which is a fast and efficient way to cover large areas. Before you go the sprayer route, however, be sure to mask the trim, windows, and everything else that you don't want painted.

Sprayers can be rented at home centers, along with ladders and scaffolding.

The cost of painting your home yourself is likely to be under $500; the cost of hiring a professional to paint it could be $6,000 to $8,000, depending on the area and season.

Just as sound and great-looking siding is critical to attractive curb appeal, a water-tight and attractive roof is equally important. Unfortunately, many first-time homeowners buy a home whose roof has only a few years left. Some appraisers require roofs to have a remaining lifespan of only three years or more. That means you'll need to start thinking of roof replacement right after you move in!

The following section lays out some typical roofing options.

ROOFS: KEEPING THE WATER OFF YOUR HEAD

A newer roof adds curb appeal and value to your home. Although putting a new roof on just prior to selling will likely not get you a dollar-for-dollar return, it will help sell the home. According to *Remodeling* magazine's 2006 "Cost vs. Value" report, nationally the average cost recouped of putting on a new roof is 73.9 percent.

As you might expect, not replacing an aging roof can easily lower the value of your home by more than the replacement cost. Once buyers see a problem area they go into a what-else-is-wrong-with-this-dump attitude, and chances of a good offer nosedive.

A far better strategy is to replace the roof or keep it in good condition before you decide to sell. Then you won't have to spend a lot of money to get the home in selling condition. And who knows, your roof may weather that once-every-500-years storm that leaks through your neighbor's roof.

INFORMATIVE ROOFING WEBSITES
www.usinspect.com/Roof/RoofMaterials.asp#Asphalt
www.nachi.org/roofs.htm
www.doityourself.com/scat/roofing
www.owenscorning.com/around/roofing/newroof.asp

www.asphaltroofing.org/resources_steep.html
www.nrca.net/consumer/fyi.aspx

There are lots of roofing options, some more expensive that others. But the first question is: How long are you likely to be in the home? Shingles are sold by the length of their warranty (e.g., 20-year, 25-year, 30-year, and more). The differences are the weight and design of the shingles.

If you're planning to move in a few years, 20-year shingles can be a good choice. But if you're planning on sticking around for a long time, the focus changes. For example, in Table 5-4, you can see that a higher initial cost often translates into a longer roof lifespan. But this is true only up to a point. Climate is a great modifier. For example, a 20-year asphalt shingle roof in a moderate climate that lasts 25 years would only last 14 years in the hot southwest or the high snowfall area of Vermont.

If you need a new roof, check out what type works best in your area. For instance, in fire-prone areas you would want to go with Class A shingles (the most fire resistant). In warm or humid climates, zinc- or copper-coated granules added to shingles can help protect against algae. Whatever type roof you need, get at least three written bids.

For all those roofs between new and nearing replacement, the following tips will help you extend their life and prevent costly water damage:

• One of the most important things you can do is inspect your roof every few months. (Do not climb or walk on the roof; use binoculars instead.)

Table 5-4. Typical roofing options.

Shingle Type	Approximate Cost	Approximate Life–Span (Depending on Climate)
20-Year Asphalt Shingles	$4,000 to $6,000	14 to 24 years
Architectural or 30-Year +	$5,000 to $8,000	26 to 35 years
Metal Roofing	$6,000 to $8,000	25 years plus
Wood Shingles	$8,500 to $10,000	20 years
Concrete Tiles	$12,000 to 15,000	25 to 40 years
Clay Tiles	$15,000 to 18,000	45 years plus
Slate	$20,000 to $30,000	50 years plus

Three things you especially want to look for with your binoculars besides birds are:

1. Brittle and curling shingles, especially along the edges
2. Protective granules wearing off, leaving bare spots on the shingles
3. Rusting or corroding flashing and cracks in sealant around pipes

• Look for gravel blowing or washing off onto the ground around tar and gravel roofs. Wear is hard to spot from the ground on these types of roofs, so it's important to get a professional roofing inspection every few years.

• After high winds or heavy rain storms, check for missing or damaged shingles.

• Make sure you have adequate attic ventilation: louvers, ridge, and soffit vents should total one square foot of ventilation for every 150 square feet of attic floor space. Moisture trapped under the roof decking can lead to mold and water damage. Check the underside of the roof decking for leaks and mold from inside the attic periodically.

• Look for rodent or squirrel damage, especially around fascia and soffit boards. If you live in squirrel or woodpecker country, adding a metal soffit and fascia covering can prevent a lot of damage.

• Make sure you have metal drip caps to protect the fascia boards under the edge of the roof.

• And a biggie that can get really ugly: a sagging ridge beam or a wavy roof. This likely means the roof and decking have to be torn off, and the damaged rafters and ridge beam need to be replaced along with any other damaged wood.

As you've probably deduced already, the battle cry for homeowners should be "keep out the water at all costs!" Vigilance will save you a lot of money in repairs and replacements.

WINDOWS DO MORE THAN LET IN LIGHT

Along with the roof, windows are your home's most costly and high-profile component. They also define the home's personality and usually match (but not always) its style. We've all seen homes where owners have upgraded and changed the window's size and type, resulting in a dramatic improvement.

ENERGY- AND MONEY-SAVING TIP

Replacing old aluminum or wood single-pane windows with energy-efficient, double-pane windows will save you serious bucks on your heating bill. You may also get a tax credit for upgrading your windows. Check out www.energystar.gov for more information.

Replacing windows may or may not give you dollar-for-dollar payback when you sell. If you have older single-pane aluminum windows and replace them with energy-efficient vinyl windows, your payback will be high. Replacing windows just to create the latest look will probably not return near your investment. Buyers often have a hard time justifying paying extra for something they consider nonessential or cosmetic.

Basically, there are two ways you can go when upgrading your home's windows:

1.   You can replace the existing windows with upgrades without altering the opening. This, of course, is the easiest and most economical way to go.

2.   You can alter the window openings for bigger or smaller windows and give your home a new look. This is an approach that you want to think through carefully to make sure the new windows are in harmony with the whole house; you may even want to consult an architect or designer. Sometimes this approach can really bump up the value of the home and justify the extra cost.

CURB-APPEAL TIP

On many homes the siding surrounds the windows so they don't have picture-type framing. When you upgrade your windows consider adding molding and trim, which can be painted or stained a different color from the siding.

If you do decide to replace windows, there are some exciting styles, coatings, and fillers that can make a big difference in your energy bills. Some typical window styles for upgrading are:

•   *Double-hung windows* have two sashes that slide up and down in the jamb. In the past a system of weights and pulleys counterbalanced the sashes. These have been replaced by pressure-fit vinyl jambs that are more weather proof and work smoother. Some models tilt inward for easier exterior-side cleaning. These are probably the oldest style and most common windows around, and with double panes they are energy efficient.

• *Casement windows* typically have hand cranks that control opening and closing. These windows are common on Craftsman, Tudor, and California Ranch style homes. Modern materials and designs have made these a good choice for replacement windows.

• *Slider windows* are a common style in homes built in the 1970s. If your home still has these single-pane aluminum sliders, replacing them with double-pane windows should be at the top of your list. The new windows are more energy efficient, and the money you save over five to ten years should easily cover the replacement cost.

• *Fixed windows* or *picture windows* are great for views and bringing light into the home. However, older single-pane windows leak a lot of energy, and replacing them with double- or even triple-pane glass should be a top priority.

One homeowner who replaced her old aluminum single-pane windows was amazed at the difference in comfort and noise levels. The large picture window in her front room had made it almost impossible to heat adequately and the traffic noise was difficult to get used to.

The owner spent $6,500 to replace all the windows in her 975-square-foot 1970s ranch-style home, including the picture window in her living room. The double-pane vinyl windows saved her about $55 a month or $660 a year in heating and cooling costs. If you divide $660 in savings into the $6,500 window replacement costs, it will take the owner about ten years to break even. However, colder climates like Minnesota or Vermont could even shorten that break-even point.

• *Bay or bow windows* are multiple windows that bump out from a wall. Typically, two double-hung windows extend out at a 45-degree angle from the wall, with a larger, fixed window in the middle. Bay windows make a great upgrade on single-level or ranch-type homes. They open up the living room or kitchen dining area to more light and room as well as add value to the home.

WINDOW-REPLACEMENT WEBSITES

www.efficientwindows.org/nfrc.cfm
www.vinyl-replacement-windows.com/vinyl-replacement-window-basics.html
www.online.consumerreports.org/Windows

www.b4ubuild.com/links/windows.shtml
www.thisoldhouse.com/toh/knowhow/tools/article/0,16417,419997,00.html

Shopping for windows isn't always easy. There are lots of options, a wide range of prices, and an incredible amount of hype. Typically, quality windows cost about $200 to $250 or more per window. A 12-window house with patio sliding door, for example, would cost around $4,500 to $6,000 installed.

The following tips will help your thread your way through the buying maze:

- Look for windows that are double-paned and argon-filled with a low E-coating, that is, ENERGY STAR–certified windows. They cost about 10 to 15 percent more but reduce energy loss by 30 to 50 percent.
- Window coatings are climate specific. You won't have the same coatings in Phoenix that you would in northern Michigan. So shop at local suppliers who know what your area needs are.
- Look for windows that have a NFRC (National Fenestration Rating Council) sticker on the window. This discloses facts about the windows that allow you to compare different models. Go to www.nfrc .org/fenestrationfacts.aspx for a complete guide to deciphering the numbers on the sticker.
- Don't buy windows from salesmen knocking on your door offering you a good deal because they happen to be in the area. Deal only with reputable window dealers or contractors.
- Double-pane insulating windows cut energy costs in hot climates as much or more than cold climates. The specific glass coating for your area will make the home much more comfortable than single-pane windows.
- Once you've decided on what windows you want, get three install bids in writing and compare them.

OTHER EXTERIOR FEATURES TO KEEP AN EYE ON

Once you've got your home watertight and storm-proof, the next area to focus on are items that are important but not critical. Important in that they need to be done to preserve curb appeal or keep from getting worse, but not critical as when you'll hear a drip, drip in the middle of the night.

Fireplaces

Fireplaces are almost a necessity for some buyers, while others could care less. How much value it gives your home depends on the area and home buyer preferences.

Still, if your home has a fireplace, it's important to keep it maintained, not only for its safe operation but to preserve your home's resale value.

INFORMATIVE FIREPLACE WEBSITES

www.homebuying.about.com/cs/fireplacesafety/a/wood_fireplace.htm
www.csia.org/homeowners.htm
www.oldhouseweb.com/stories/detailed/10151.shtml

On homes ten years old or older, start out by getting a fireplace inspection (wood burning stoves included). It's important to know what condition your fireplace is in. Typically this will cost around $50 for an inspection and $250 for cleaning. If the firebrick liner or metal flue is damaged or worn out, you'll need to replace it. Depending on the type wood you burn, how often you build a fire and the climate, liners usually last anywhere from 12 to 50 years. Cost to replace liners and structural repairs can run from $1,500 to $3,000.

To keep your fireplace in top condition and enjoy it safely, check out the following tips:

- Use the fireplace for short-duration fires, five hours or less.
- Open glass doors or vents to allow air to be drawn up to cool the chimney.
- Keep screens closed to prevent sparks from jumping out onto the carpeting.
- Never leave a fire unattended when children are around.
- Open a window when using the fireplace so air can circulate up the chimney.
- Make sure your chimney has a cap to keep out rodents, birds, and nests, and a spark arrestor to keep sparks from torching your neighbor's roof.
- Fireplace coals can remain hot long after the fire has burned down. Remove ashes with a metal shovel or scoop (never a vacuum) and store in a metal container away from anything flammable.
- If you're a heavy fireplace user, have a chimney sweep check it each fall before you use it. This is important because obstructions or prob-

lems can cause carbon monoxide to back up into the home, and that's something you don't wake up from. Adding carbon monoxide alarms should be a must near the furnace room and close to fireplaces.

- Smoke detectors in every room are a building code requirement in most states. If you have an older home that doesn't have them, they're cheap and easy to install, and they run off 9-volt batteries that have to be replaced about every six months.

- If you convert your fireplace to use another type of fuel (natural gas, wood, propane, pellet, etc.) make sure your conversion meets local codes and have it installed or inspected by a pro. There's no room for error here because carbon monoxide (CO) fumes from an improper install are lethal.

Swimming Pools

In some parts of the country, swimming pools are as important as the family dog, and a home may be a hard sell without one. In other areas, a home may be a hard sell with one.

Regardless of what area you live in, if you have a pool, it's a big investment. To keep that investment in good shape, good maintenance is a must. For most new pool owners the first step is to find a pool maintenance contractor. Likely, the previous owners used a maintenance company, and if they were happy with the service, you may want to continue with the same outfit. Because pool maintenance is a highly competitive business, you can be sure they'll be contacting you soon after you move in. Otherwise, use the standard procedure for finding a contractor: minimum of three written bids, testimonials, and personal interviews to find one you're comfortable with.

INFORMATIVE POOL-OWNER WEBSITES

www.home.howstuffworks.com/swimming-pool.htm
www.cdc.gov/healthyswimming
www.swimmingpools101.com
www.home.comcast.net/~hot_tub
www.learnaboutpools.com

You'll also want to contact your homeowner's insurance provider and make sure you're covered for additional liability on the pool.

Garage Doors

Garage doors are an important part of your home's curb appeal and should be maintained in as good a condition as the rest of the exterior. That means keeping the opening system, door, and bottom weather strips in good order. This is important not only to prevent energy loss but to maintain home security.

GARAGE-DOOR INFORMATION WEBSITES

www.hometips.com/cs-protected/guides/garage.html
www.cpsc.gov/cpscpub/pubs/523.html
www.nhc.noaa.gov/HAW2/english/retrofit/garage_doors.shtml
www.home.howstuffworks.com/how-to-repair-a-garage-door.htm

If your garage door is beyond maintenance and it's time to replace, consider these shopping tips:

• The first decision is the style; obviously it has to fit your home's style. In other words, a carriage-house design probably won't look good on a California Ranch-style home. You want the style and color to fit the home.

• The next decision is the color and texture. That too must blend or contrast with the home. For ideas look at new homes and see what other homeowners have done.

• It may cost slightly more, but shop for doors that have sections made of wood or steel that include a sandwich of foam insulation. Insulating the garage door results in significant energy savings.

When you're shopping for a door, you'll find many options; it can get confusing. Table 5-5 can help.

To new homeowners it may seem that maintenance and upgrading are a never ending hassle. And to a certain extent that's true. Although it's nice to be able to call the super or landlord to take care of problems, there's much more satisfaction in acquiring the skills and know-how to maintain your own home.

The appeal of fixing up a house, decorating it, and making it uniquely theirs is what motivates most new homeowners to fire the landlord. And the good news is, it gets better and more fun the more you learn and experiment.

The checklist in Table 5-6 is designed to help you keep the outside of your home in good condition. After a while, looking for problem areas becomes automatic as you gain experience and join the ranks of seasoned homeowners.

Table 5-5. Typical garage door options.

Option	Pros	Cons	Approximate Cost Installed
Wood	Can be customized, natural wood look, unlimited styles.	Like wood siding, it needs refinishing. Costly.	$1,700 to $5,000
Vinyl	Light weight, can be customized, won't rot, paintable.	Dark paint colors may peel.	$1,500 to 2,500
Steel	Durable, light weight, good insulation, damaged sections replaceable.	Cheaper look than wood or vinyl. If painted, must be maintained.	$750 to $1,500
Composite	Made from wood fibers and resin, won't rot, sections can be replaced.	Once painted, it has to be maintained to look good.	$750 to $1,000
Adding Windows	Adds curb appeal and lets light into the garage.	Adds cost and maintenance.	$100 to $500
Adding Insulation	Prevents energy leaks.	Adds cost.	$50 to $150
New Track and Operator	Replace if old, noisy, and lacking safety features.	None.	$200 to $500

Table 5-6. Exterior seasonal and maintenance checklist.

Item	Action Needed
Electrical Wires	Trim tree limbs that are threatening power lines to the electrical service entrance so that ice storms, winds, and heavy snow don't down a line.
Outside Electrical Panel	Check outside electrical panel for wasp nests or loose wires.
Cracks in Concrete or Asphalt	Fill all cracks before freezing weather sets in so water doesn't infiltrate and freeze, causing more damage. Home centers sell concrete and asphalt crack sealers that prevent this.
Retaining Walls	Make sure there are no bulges or failing areas that can break loose in a heavy snow or rain.
Wood Porches	Check all the wood for rot, failed paint, and loose boards. Repair immediately to prevent further damage.
Siding	Look for areas that need caulking. Check for signs of paint failure or where water can get behind the siding.
Soffits and Fascia	Look for peeling paint, loose boards, rodent or bird damage. Look for anywhere water is going where it shouldn't be.
Around Chimneys	Make sure flashing and siding-to-chimney contact is in watertight condition. Caulk or replace flashing if deteriorated.
Gutters	Make sure laterals and downspouts are free of debris and are not leaking. Attach extensions to channel water away from the house.
Foundations	Look for cracks or places where water can get in, such as utility pipes and wiring.
Termites	If you live in termite country, get a professional inspection to make sure your home isn't being devoured by the ravenous bugs.
Grade	Look at the grade around the foundation and make sure it routes water away rather than into the crawl space or basement.
Roof	Look for missing shingles, cracks in flashing around pipes, and valleys.
Moss	If you find moss, eliminate it with a fungicide or 1 part bleach to 2 parts water.
Well	Have the water tested yearly for contamination.
Septic System	Have it pumped as needed or set up a maintenance contract with a reputable dealer. Check for soggy ground or lush plant growth around the septic field. That could mean a full tank or a failing system.
Sump Pump	Test by pouring water into the well; pump should turn on automatically.
Weather Stripping	Check around windows and doors for wear.
Roof Vent Pipes	Make sure they are free of leaves, bird nests, and other debris.

CHAPTER 6

YOUR HOME'S LANDSCAPING
AND CURB APPEAL

Curb appeal to a home is what packaging is to the products you buy. The better it's packaged, the more successful it is. Even if you don't plan on selling for awhile—the national average for living in a home is slightly over seven years—it's critical to keep your landscaping and yard in top condition. You'll not only enjoy your home more, but when the time does come to sell you won't have to pay a lot to catch up.

You don't have to have a green thumb to have a great yard and enjoy it. Like decorating the interior, you can create your own little world and have fun doing it. True, there are a few new skills to develop, but they're not difficult.

This chapter gives you some basic tips on how to make your yard look good and keep it that way. Still, you'll probably want to take landscaping your yard to a higher level by reading magazines, landscaping books, and checking out new subdivisions for cutting-edge ideas.

To get you started, some important tips covered in this chapter are:

✓   Dressing up your yard for maximum curb appeal

✓   Creating and keeping an attractive lawn

✓   Using trees, bushes, and hedges in your landscaping

✓   Keeping driveways, walks, and fences in good condition

We all want to make a good impression on friends and family when they come to visit us, and a good way to do this is with killer curb appeal.

HOW TO CREATE KILLER CURB APPEAL

Step one is to walk across the street from your home with a digital camera and a note pad. Take pictures of your yard from several angles and note the problems you see.

Examples of problems to look for are:

- Balance and symmetry. Does one side have something that makes the front view look unbalanced? For example, are there trees, large bushes, hedges, or a fence running along one side with nothing on the other side to balance it?
- Is there a utility box on the property line that creates a distraction? Some streets with underground power lines have large transformer boxes a few feet from the curb.
- Are there problem areas that need attention, such as an old fence, bare or dead spots in the lawn, or out-of-control bushes and trees?
- Are there foundation bushes that are not trimmed below the windows and out just a couple of feet from the home?
- Do your driveway and walks have cracks or spalling (deteriorating) surfaces?
- Are there sunken walkway sections, especially where they tie into the porch? These can also be serious safety hazards.
- How do your curb appeal photos look? Eventually if you put your home on the market, similar photos on a website are likely to be a buyer's first introduction to your home. If there are glaring problems, or one side of the house is particularly ugly, you should address these first.

Once you've put together a problems list, order them in a way that you can tackle and complete them. For example, if you were planning on selling the home soon, time would be an important factor and the order wouldn't matter too much, just so you get it all done. But if your project is to make your home look its best, then order the list by cost, by what you can do personally, or by what's important to you.

Step two is to develop a plan from your list, pull on the gloves, and have fun.

INTERESTING CURB-APPEAL WEBSITES

www.hgtv.com/hgtv/pac_ctnt_988/text/0,,HGTV_22056_32482,00.html
www.homebuying.about.com/cs/sellerarticles/a/curb_appeal.htm
www.popularmechanics.com/how_to_central/home_clinic/1548397.html
www.dannylipford.com/home_improvement.php?cat = lawn
www.the-landscape-design-site.com/directory

LANDSCAPING BASICS

To plan an attractive organized yard, you don't have to spend big bucks to hire a landscape architect. The key is to develop a simple plan and gradually add to it over time. Don't make it too complicated or overwhelming.

Some homeowners like to start out drawing a to-scale landscaping plan of their yard on a large sheet of graph paper. Others prefer to buy a software program and plan with a screen and mouse. If you go the software route, there are many programs on the market—some good, others not so good. Two programs worth checking out are *Your Complete Landscape and Garden Designer* and *Better Homes and Gardens Landscaping and Deck Designer*. One advantage of a software program is that you can import photos of your yard and see how changes impact your landscaping ideas.

Some basics for developing your landscaping plan are:

- Create a base plan. Draw an scale outline of the property on a large sheet of graph paper showing the dimensions, where the house is located, easements, setback distances from other homes, sidewalks, and streets.
- Add in walls, walks, fences, decks, and other appurtenances.
- Draw in drainage patterns, sources of noise or privacy problems, and views you want to preserve.
- Attach an overlay of tracing paper to the base plan and pencil in the changes or additions that you want to make.

- Try to blend the finished landscaping with the neighborhood. Curb appeal is lost when your home and landscaping are out of character with the rest of the neighborhood.

When you're working on your landscaping plan, keep in mind the following seven design elements that every landscaping should have:

1. Good landscape design starts with composition. Trees, shrubs, flower beds, and walks should fix together like pieces in a puzzle. Landscaping features should be grouped into related components. For example, an elongated area enclosed by concrete curbing could have a grouping of three trees on one end. Colorful flowers could be planted in the middle, and another grouping of smaller trees (flowering fruit trees, for instance) could anchor the other end. The key is to create a sense of balance.

2. When you stand on the curb looking at a home's landscaping and feel there's something missing or isn't quite right, it's usually from lack of balance. Balance is created by placing trees, flower gardens, fences, bushes, and hedges in harmony with each other. When you develop a landscaping plan first, you can move these elements around on paper (or screen) until you achieve a balance. If you start planting without a plan, as many homeowners do, achieving balance is difficult.

3. Scale is the next element to creating killer curb appeal. Driving around any subdivision in the country, it would appear that most homeowners ignore scale when planting trees and shrubs. They don't realize that trees and plants grow up and that the cute fir tree planted by the house isn't going to stay that way. The home in Figure 6-1 shows what happens when a homeowner forgets that a blue spruce can grow up and create problems. If this home were to go on the market, the owner would need to remove the tree to get top dollar.

4. In nature there's a natural ratio of 3 to 5 (often called the Golden Mean or ratio) that resonates with most people. Because we identify with this ratio and find it comfortable, it's commonly used in architecture, advertising layouts and countless other applications. In landscaping your yard, you can use this ratio to design flower beds, plant groupings and so on. For example, if you were to design an garden area enclosed by curbing using this 3:5 ratio, the size could be 9 feet by 15 feet, or 12 feet by 20 feet, and so on. (In other words, 3 feet × 5 feet doubled is 6 feet × 10 feet, tripled it's 9 feet × 15 feet, and so on.) This is also why you often see plants and trees grouped in threes and fives.

Figure 6-1.

5.   Because a yard with only grass can be boring, it's important to add color. This is a good opportunity to add your favorite colors to the landscaping. Flowers, ground cover, window boxes, and planters are a great way to add colorful personality to your yard.

6.   Another important attribute of landscape design is texture. A good way to use this is to group like-textured plants together. For instance, you wouldn't plant a red lacey-leafed maple next to scrub pines.

7.   If all the landscaping elements discussed thus far are used, the result should be harmony. Your yard will not only be attractive, but you and your guests will enjoy being there. As Realtors are fond of saying, it has emotional appeal.

Once you've got your landscaping plan put together, the first step in implementing it is to make sure the lawn is thick and green. It's the backdrop for the rest of the landscaping.

However, if you live in the arid southwest, the rules are quite a bit different. Instead of lawns, it's sand, rocks, and drought-resistant plants. Colorful flowers in planters and pots give you a great opportunity to be creative. The same design principles apply; only the medium changes.

For the rest of the lawnmower-owning homeowners, it all starts with the turf.

LAWN CARE 101

The two house hunters had looked at over a dozen homes that day and found none of them appealing. Some houses had yards that looked like they would support a buffalo or two, while others were just dirt. The shoppers were nearing the end of the list when they drove up to a home with a great-looking lawn.

Not having time before getting transferred to do much more than put in the lawn, the owners had decided to make it a selling point at the urging of their agent. It was a carpet of manicured lush green. The buyers took a quick look through the home, walked across the lawn, and told their agent to write up a full-price offer; they didn't want to chance losing it. As the buyers said later, "The yard doesn't have any trees or other landscaping, but that's good. We can do what we want because the hard part is done."

LAWN-CARE WEBSITES

www.yardcare.com
www.allaboutlawns.com
www.lawn-care-tips.com/lawncaretips.html
www.backyardgardener.com/lawn
www.eartheasy.com/grow_lawn_care.htm
www.gardening.cornell.edu/lawn/lawncare/index.html

Many people feel intimidated by putting in a lawn or making an existing one the envy of the neighborhood. The following tips will help you turn brown into lush green:

- For a killer lawn you need several inches of well-drained, noncompacted soil. Otherwise you'll have to bring in about four inches of top soil and mix in organic material. Cow, chicken, or turkey manure work well, as does leaf compost and peat moss.
- Testing your soil's pH level is an important step. If the soil is too acid or too alkaline, you won't get good results. If it tests acid (less than 7) or alkaline (over 7) you may need to compensate. Typically, lawns thrive best on a pH level between 6 and 7 or slightly acidic. Soil testing kits are available at garden centers, or in some areas from the U.S. Department of Agriculture, whose website is:
www.nrcs.usda.gov/feature/backyard/NutMgt.html

- The soil should be raked into a smooth seedbed, with no rocks or compacted areas. Any drainage problems need to be corrected so a rainstorm won't wash out your new lawn.

Once the seedbed is prepared, there are three ways you can go:

1. The most economical way is to buy the seeds and spread them yourself using a wheeled spreader or hand-cranked broadcaster, which can also be used to apply fertilizer when the lawn is established. Spring and fall are the best times to plant lawn seed. Follow the directions on the seed package for best coverage.

2. *Hydro-seeding*, though more expensive than applying seeds yourself, is fast and efficient. Typically the cost is between $250 and $400 for a 1,000 to 3,000 square-foot lawn. With this process a slurry of grass seed, wood fibers, and fertilizer is sprayed on the seedbed. You keep the area moist, and in a few weeks you have a lawn. Check under lawn installation in the yellow pages for hydro-seeders in your area.

3. Slightly more expensive than hydro-seeding is buying live sod from a sod farm. A big advantage is you have an instant lawn that's ready for the kids to play on in a few days. It's also a quick way to upgrade your lawn when you're planning to sell. Depending on the grass type and where you live, sod delivered on a pallet typically costs $.25 to $.40 per square foot.

Regardless of the way you go, it's important to keep the lawn watered frequently until it's completely established.

FERTILIZER FACTS

Most areas fertilize their lawns three to four times a year. A local nursery can give you the best mix for your lawn type. Bagged fertilizers have labels with three numbers, such as 20-10-5.
The first number gives you the nitrogen content. A higher number means more nitrogen.
The second number is phosphorus, which is needed for a healthy root system.
The last number is potash, which provides amino acids and proteins for lush plant growth.

Edging

The next step in taking your lawn and yard to the next level is installing edging. This is the icing on the cake: It not only gives your lawn a manicured look, but makes it easier to maintain. There are several ways you can create great looking edging:

- Use a gas- or electric-powered edger to cut clean lines between lawn, walks, driveways, and flowerbeds.
- Hire a professional landscaper to curb around lawns and enclose flowerbeds. You can even get several different patterns and colors to create a customized look. Curbing costs typically between $2 to $3 a running foot.
- Install vinyl, wood, or metal edging you can buy at home and garden centers. Bricks, pavers, and narrow strips of crushed stone or gravel also work well.

*   *   *

By this time you've probably spent a lot of time and money getting your lawn up to speed, or if you're a new homeowner you undoubtedly look at the mortgage balance and feel every blade of grass is worth a lot of money.

The following ten *Do's* and *Don'ts* summarize and show you how to protect your investment and keep it green.

1. Testing Your Soil

You'll want to know the levels of potassium, magnesium, calcium, sulfur, nitrogen, and organic matter. The U.S. Department of Agriculture has county extension offices that can direct you. For the office nearest you, check out www.csrees.usda.gov/extension.

SOIL-TESTING WEBSITES

www.outsidepride.com/store/catalog/Soil-Test-Kits-p-1-c-268.html
www.agr.state.nc.us/cyber/kidswrld/plant/soiltest.htm
www.ohioline.osu.edu/hyg-fact/1000/1132.html
www.drgoodearth.com/?src = overture

2. Mowing at the Proper Height

Each time you mow some of the plant leaf is removed. If you remove too much, the plant can't produce the nutrients it needs to survive. Mowing too short also weakens, thins out the grass blades, and allows weeds to gain a foothold.

Every ⅛-inch increase in mowing height increases the leaf surface 30 percent. In the Northern states where grasses are predominately bluegrass, fescue, and rye grasses, mow 3 inches or higher during mid to late spring and early fall. During the hot mid-summer weeks setting the mower blade 4 inches high helps your lawn get through the heat.

Southern grasses, namely St. Augustine and bahia, should be mowed during summer and early fall at 3 to 4 inches. Bermuda, centipede, and zoysia grasses can tolerate 2- to 3-inch mower settings.

3. Cutting Too Much at Once

Lawns should be mowed frequently. Cutting too much off in one mowing, however, forces the grass to put all its energy into replacing lost leaf area. This stops vital root growth and food storage.

Follow the ⅓ rule: Mow as often as needed, but don't remove more than a third of the grass blade. In other words, if you mow at 3 inches, the grass length shouldn't be more than 4½ inches.

4. Watering Wisely

Many homeowners with automatic sprinkler systems set them to come on every day for 10 or 15 minutes. Though frequent, the water output isn't enough to penetrate into the root zone where it's needed. As a result, the plants tend to develop shallow root systems that dry out quickly during hot weather.

To give your lawn the right amount of water where it does the most good, set your sprinkler's timer to water for an hour or so. Test the water penetration by pushing a spade about six inches into the soil. If it's moist down to that depth, you're on the right track.

Water heavily once a week, or twice if the weather is hot and windy. Early morning is the best time to water to minimize evaporation loss. Don't over-water, that can be as damaging as too little water. If the grass becomes wilted with a bluish hue, it needs water ASAP.

5. Keeping Mower Blades Sharp

A dull mower blade shreds instead of cutting. This can leave ragged grass ends with an unattractive gray color, and it also invites insect problems.

Start the mowing season with a sharp blade and resharpen whenever it starts to dull. Check the lawn for sticks, rocks, or anything that will nick the blade or cause a safety problem before you mow. Some homeowners have two blades so when one becomes dull they can replace it and drop off the dull one to be professionally sharpened. (Hey, Saturdays are too important for lawn-mowing downtime!)

Mulching blades are especially sensitive to maintaining a good edge because they must slice grass several times. Unless you're good at sharpening, it's best to have these blades re-edged by a professional.

6. Clippings

If you mow frequently and use a mulching blade, leave the clippings on the lawn where they will break down and reduce the need for fertilizer. It's also more environmentally responsible to keep as much material out of landfills as possible.

If you wait too long between mowings and end up cutting grass longer than an inch, the cuttings can bunch up on top of the lawn. This results in unsightly rows of brown grass. Unfortunately, whenever you let the lawn grow too long the only way to prevent these rows of dead grass is to use the bag attachment. You can feel guilty over this and vow not to let it happen again, but then, when the fish are biting. . . .

7. Improving Your Soil Quality

Good quality soil is highly active with earthworms, microbes, and other organisms that break down clippings and improve soil texture. It's a big, complex world at the root level, which you need to maintain at a healthy level.

Unfortunately, using too much insecticide, fungicide, fertilizer, and snow-melting salt can cause problems with these beneficial organisms. To keep your soil healthy:

- Use soil activators (available at all garden centers) that increase the level of beneficial organisms in your lawn.
- When you need to use insecticides and fungicides, treat only the area affected to prevent damaging unaffected parts of your lawn. Depending on the problem, you may be able to use nonchemical remedies.
- If the underlying soil is starting to compact, hire an aerating service or rent an aerating machine. Aerating machines punch 2-inch-deep holes into the turf every 6 inches and remove a small plug of soil. This

allows water and nutrients to penetrate into the root zone. Spring is the best time to aerate a lawn.

8. Using Fertilizer

Many fertilizers are synthetic and high in nitrogen. They're fast-acting and can overstimulate plant growth. This weakens the plants and opens to door to fungus and insect problems.

For most lawns, organic and synthetic slow-release fertilizers work best. They release nutrients slowly and reduce the chance of burning (killing the grass). If you want to use organic products, manure, fish meal, and kelp work well.

Fertilize no more than three times a year and don't apply more than 1 pound of nitrogen per 1,000 square feet of lawn at a time.

Fertilizing at the Right Time

Timing is important; if the grass is brown, weeds will flourish and take over the lawn.

Fertilize Northern lawns in early fall and again later on when growth has stopped but before the lawn has turned brown. This helps nurture the grass through the winter months and gives it a boost for the spring growing season. The next feeding should be in the spring, just before it gets hot.

Southern lawns thrive in summer heat and can be fertilized then. Best times for this climate are early spring, summer, and early fall.

10. Keeping Thatch Under Control

Thatch is the matting of dead grass, roots, and plant matter above the soil surface. It forms a barrier that prevents water and fertilizer from penetrating into the root zone. This makes your lawn a target for all those critters that prey on grass.

Three things you can do to minimize the buildup of thatch are:

1. As discussed earlier, aeration can break through thatch. However this is a temporary solution, because thatch needs to break down and decompose on a continuing basis to keep your lawn healthy.
2. A long-term solution is to encourage earthworms and microbes to take up residence in the thatch zone and be happy. You do this by maintaining the pH level of the soil between 6.5 and 7 (7 is the neu-

tral zone; neither acid or alkaline) and watering on a consistent schedule.

3. If the thatch is over ½ inch you can rent a power rake or dethatcher. Be aware that mechanical raking can be destructive because lawn roots that are growing in the thatch zone will tear out easily.

   Because over-seeding is usually required after power raking, it's best to go this route in late August for optimum seed germination.

USEFUL WEBSITES ABOUT THATCH

www.urbanext.uiuc.edu/lawnchallenge/lesson5.html
www.extension.umn.edu/distribution/horticulture/DG1123.html
www.uky.edu/Ag/Entomology/entfacts/trees/ef402.htm
www.ohric.ucdavis.edu/Newsltr/CTC/ctcv34_1.pdf

When you get your lawn green and when the worms, friendly bugs, and microbes are happy, it's time to turn your attention to bigger game.

TREES AND SHRUBS

One huge problem many homeowners have is allowing their landscaping to get out of control. Foundation bushes grow up and cover windows, and trees planted too close to the house cause siding and roofing damage. Other curb-appeal destroyers are too many trees and bushes in front of the home giving it a back-to-nature appearance.

Ideally, trees should frame a home, not block its view from the street or prevent light from entering the home. Rooms that are dark and dreary from lack of light substantially lower a home's value.

INTERESTING GUIDES TO PRUNING AND CHIPPING

www.aggie-horticulture.tamu.edu/extension/pruning/pruning.html
www.na.fs.fed.us/spfo/pubs/howtos/ht_prune/prun001.htm
www.extension.umn.edu/distribution/horticulture/DG0628.html
www.arborday.org/Trees/pruning
www.extension.umn.edu/distribution/naturalresources/DD3949.html

If your trees and shrubs have made your yard look like a jungle, taming them will do wonders for your curb appeal and pride of homeownership. The following tips will get you started:

•   Note what hedges, bushes, and trees obscure your home and need to be trimmed or removed. Trimming is a big project because piles of cuttings build up quickly. You'll need to arrange for a large rental dumpster or other means of getting the refuse to a landfill. Another more green approach is to rent a chipper and turn the cuttings into mulch.

•   Don't feel you're damaging plants by pruning excess growth, it usually benefits most trees and shrubs. Older, overgrown plants may be reinvigorated if they are thinned to allow more light and air.

•   For thinning shrubs, find a bud facing the direction you want a branch to grow and cut above it. If you pinch or cut off growing tips in the spring, it will make the shrub bushier and more compact, something you may want to do with foundation plants.

•   Foundation plants should be trimmed down so they don't grow above the bottom window sill. Nor should any tree limbs obscure the view from any windows.

•   Leave about a 2-foot space between the house and any plants. You want to allow air and light to circulate and to discourage mold and fungus growth on the siding.

•   To get ideas of how plants can be used to increase your home's attraction, check out new homes and subdivisions. Builders often hire professionals to landscape their model homes. Note the type of plants these landscapers use and how they're grouped. Also, as you drive around different subdivisions, notice what you like and don't like about what other homeowners have done with their yards.

Staying on top of landscaping isn't difficult, it just takes a consistent effort to stay ahead of the plant's growing cycles and being aware that at certain times you'll need to get out the pruning shears. The following are the five most common pruning mistakes homeowners make:

1.   Never top or remove large parts of the tree. It can either kill the tree or create an ugly tree with limbs trying to grow out the trunk to compensate. One appraiser estimated that a well-placed mature tree is worth anywhere from $1,000 to $10,000, depending on the area.
2.   Avoid pruning more than a quarter of the live branches at one time,

or more than a third in a year. Stimulating too much growth creates additional work for you later on. This is why letting bushes get out of control and then having a pruning party is counter-productive.

3. Improper pruning leaves stubs too far from a dormant bud or another branch. These stubs invite decay and disease.

4. Never coat pruning wounds with paint, shellac, or tar. This can damage trees by holding in moisture and causing decay.

5. Perhaps the biggest mistake is not pruning at all, and letting everything grow until it reaches a panic point. These homeowners devalue their homes and the rest of the neighborhood as well.

In one extreme case, a homeowner refused to mow the lawn or take care of his yard. The neighbors got together and offered to do it for him on weekends when they did theirs.

Yes, the neighbors could have gone the legal route, but that probably wouldn't have solved the problem. Because it was a small yard, the homeowners along the street agreed that as long as the slob neighbor agreed to it, spending a few minutes every week or so mowing his lawn was their best short-term solution. (It's been going on now for six years!)

To their credit, the homeowners in the neighborhood took a pragmatic approach: They recognized that an out-of-control yard can adversely affect the value of the entire neighborhood.

FROM GREEN TO ASPHALT AND CONCRETE

Along with landscaping, driveways and walks are a big part of what makes up curb appeal. You can have a great a great lawn, but if the driveway surface is weathered and flakey (spalling), it calls attention to an unsolved problem. Lush lawn and flower beds won't even be noticed by visitors or buyers if they see a driveway with cracks, holes, or other signs of neglect.

If you want to know how important driveways are to your home's value, check out what builders are installing at new homes, such as concrete stampings that look like brick, or stone along with added color and weather sealing.

MORE INFORMATION ON ASPHALT DRIVEWAYS

www.hotmix.org/driveways.php
www.drivewayimpressions.com
www.pavementpro.org/homeowners_questions.htm
www.naturalhandyman.com/iip/infdrivewaysealer/infdrivewaysealer.shtm

Asphalt makes attractive driveways and has a few advantages over concrete. For example:

- Asphalt is more flexible than concrete and can be installed over more uneven surfaces.
- In cold climates asphalt's dark color absorbs heat better than concrete.
- Asphalt does not require formwork or long curing times
- If it's damaged, asphalt is easy to repair.
- For long runs over 25 feet, asphalt can cost much less than concrete or brick.

However, you can't put in an asphalt driveway on the cheap and expect it hold up. Some do's are:

- Asphalt drives need to be installed by a paving contractor. It's not a do-it-yourself project because of the large equipment needed.
- You should install 6 inches of road base gravel for the asphalt base. Some homeowners try to shortcut this step, which eventually causes the driveway to sink in sections or develop potholes.
- Just like a road or highway, the driveway needs a 1 percent slope or crown to let water drain off. This is especially important in cold climates so that water won't penetrate the asphalt and freeze.
- Depending on the climate and usage, your driveway needs to be resealed every few years to keep it looking good and preventing water from penetrating. Always use a reputable contractor. Cost should be in the $250 to $400 range.

CONSUMER ALERT

For some reason scams involving asphalt resealing or repair are too common. Don't go with a door-to-door salesman, and don't fall for the "leftover mix" scam. Also beware of a salesman who:

- Pushes you for a quick decision.
- Offers you a better deal if you pay cash.
- Offers no written contract.
- Whose offer appears too good to be true.

Concrete is another great driveway option. It's durable and there are lots of options if you want to jazz it up. It can be tinted, embedded with decorative stone and brick, textured, formed to look like bricks, tile, slate, and so on.

One problem many homeowners have is not keeping their concrete driveways clean and free of oil stains. Few things can detract from curb appeal more than dark stains on the driveway from oil-leaking vehicles. There are number of oil-stain-removing products available from auto parts stores. For an environmentally friendly cleaner, try a solution of baking soda and water. Make a paste, apply it to the stain and cover with plastic for a day or two, and then rinse.

If you have a concrete driveway and it's not sealed, this is a project that should go to the top of your to-do list. Sealing a driveway requires just two easy steps:

1. Thoroughly wash the concrete surface with a TSP (tri-sodium phosphate) solution according to package directions.
2. Apply a concrete sealer (available from home centers) with a paint roller, squeegee, or sprayer according to product directions and allow to dry.

Sealing a driveway can extend its life considerably because it prevents water from penetrating the concrete—especially through cracks and seams—and freezing.

Cracks and minor problems should be fixed promptly before the damage gets worse. Spending less than $25 for patching material beats spending several thousand dollars replacing a driveway destroyed by weather.

The following steps outline how to repair minor damage:

•   Remove the damaged and loose concrete with a cold chisel. After you've cleaned out all the damaged material, bevel or undercut the edges of the opening you've made with the chisel slanted slightly away from you. This is so the patching material will flow under the edge and create a more stable patch.
•   Clean and hose out the area you're patching. Sponge up the water in the damaged area, but leave it a little damp.
•   In a small bucket, mix a cement slurry (pancake-batter consistency) of Portland cement and water. Thoroughly coat the area you're patching with this slurry; it acts like a primer for the main patch filling.
•   In a large bucket mix one part Portland cement, three parts sand, and enough water to make a stiff paste. Pack this into the area you're

patching with a putty knife or small trowel. Mix up the filler to make sure you don't leave any air pockets.

- Level the cement fill with a straight-edged trowel and allow the patch to set for about an hour. Then float or trowel the finish to match the surrounding surface.
- Allow the patch to set for a couple of hours and then cover with plastic. The cover will stay on for about a week while patch cures. Meanwhile weigh down the plastic so it will stay in place.
- The final step is to sprinkle a little water on the patch daily to keep it moist while it cures.

In lieu of buying a bag of Portland cement and a bag of sand, you may be able to get a bag of concrete patch mix; just add water like to a cake mix and you're ready to go.

CHECK OUT THESE PATCHING AND RESURFACING WEBSITES

www.askthebuilder.com/ConcreteDefects.shtml
www.acehardware.com/sm-repairing-and-patching-concrete—bg-
    1283399.html
www.pavepatch.com/?gclid = CMqI0vW9sYkCFQLYYgod7hneVQ
www.concretenetwork.com/jim_peterson/spray_top.htm
www.interstateproducts.com/concrete.htm

Asphalt driveways need resealing every few years. You can hire a professional for a few hundred dollars, or you can buy sealer at any home center; it's a messy job, though. Also available are tubes of crack sealer you use in a caulking gun. Make sure water doesn't penetrate underneath the asphalt and freeze, causing the familiar potholes you bounce through on roads.

Patching Steps and Walkways

Concrete steps and walks are high-visibility items. No one can enter your home without noticing problem areas. Chipped corners and damaged steps are ugly—not something you want messing up your curb appeal.

You've really got two options: 1) Hire a contractor to tear out the problem and redo, or 2) if it isn't too bad, save a lot of money and patch the holes and chipped steps yourself. If you go the number two route, you can save a lot of money, and it isn't that difficult a job.

Remember the formula for patching the driveway: one part Portland cement mixed with three parts sand and enough water to make a stiff paste? This same mix and technique works for damaged walkways.

Repairing steps and porches uses this same concrete mix, but the technique is different. For fixing damage on the step edge:

- Using a cold chisel and small sledge hammer (don't use a claw hammer for this, remove the damaged concrete from the stair lip back far enough to get all the damaged area. The chipped out area will look like a rough L-shaped channel along the front of the step. Spray the area you chipped out with a hose to clean out all the debris.
- Make a plywood form the height of the step riser and brace it against step face with 2 × 4s to hold the repair mix in place. (Duct tape also works well for holding the form in place.)
- Mix a batch of concrete mix and a small amount of the slurry mix. Coat the area to be repaired with slurry mix.
- Fill in the channel you chipped out behind the plywood form with concrete mix and smooth it with a trowel so it's even with the rest of the step.
- Let the mix set up for about an hour. Then, using a concrete edging trowel (a trowel with a small lip it for edging concrete) create an edge on the step that matches the others.
- Keep the patch moist by lightly spraying it with a hose and keeping it covered for about a week until it cures.

Chipped corners are fixed the same way: Make a plywood form to contain the patch and use the above procedure. In fact, you can repair most chips and cracks in concrete with this technique.

One problem that's more difficult to solve is getting the new patch to match the weathered concrete. If it's the porch you've done a lot of restoration on, the best solution is stain or paint the entire porch to match. Paint stores have a wide variety of concrete coatings. Light grey and tan, for example, are attractive.

Other solutions that have proven successful—depending on your climate—are covering the surface with tile, slate, wood decking, or other durable materials. One enterprising homeowner rented a saw with a concrete cutting blade and thin-sliced brick about 1/2-inch thick. He then laid the red brick slices like tile over the walkway and porch using white grout. An ugly stained and cracked porch became an attractive focal point for the entryway. The only limit is making sure it looks good and is durable.

Dry-Laid Walkways

A popular alternative to concrete walkways is laying pavers over a sand bed. Home centers sell these concrete pavers in a wide variety of interlocking and lattice patterns. The lattice patterns are sometimes installed so grass will grow up through the openings creating an interesting walkway or RV parking pad.

The decision you need to make when putting in a paving system is the type of edging you want to use. Dry-laid pavers need a edging system to contain the pavers and keep them from slipping apart. Typical edging materials are brick, treated wood, concrete edging, metal, or plastic. Local home centers usually carry various edging options that work with their pavers.

Dry-laid pavers are a great way to go for homeowners who want a DIY project that doesn't require a lot of equipment or expense. It's easy to put in a good looking walkway. The steps are:

1. Outline the walkway you want with chalk, paint, or a chalk-line and stakes. It can be straight or curvy, and you can add bump-outs for benches, yard lights, a flagpole, potted plants, or whatever.
2. Remove any grass and excavate the walkway about 10 inches deep so you end up with a smooth bed free of rocks, roots, or debris.
3. Install the edging.
4. Install a bed of gravel or crushed stone about four inches deep for a base.
5. Lay landscaping fabric over the base. Many homeowners skip this step and end up with weeds and grass growing up through the pavers.
6. Over the bed and fabric lay about two inches of sand.
7. Lay the pavers on the sand bed and tamp down lightly with a rented tamping tool. Once you've got the walkway the way you want it, tamp sand into the joints or spaces between the pavers.

You can also use this system to create patios, garden walkways, or edging along fences, driveways, and the foundation. Your imagination is the only limit to the projects you can create.

FENCES AND HEDGES

Another important component of landscaping and curb appeal is fencing or other dividers. It's often said that good fences make good neighbors; sometimes that's true but other times they become flash points for neighborly mis-understandings.

Some important things you should know about fences and boundaries are:

- Fence heights and setbacks are often regulated by zoning laws. Before you build or renovate a fence, check with zoning. Many times existing fences don't conform to current laws.
- Materials and fence type may be regulated by historical commissions, homeowner's associations, deed restrictions, and subdivision cove-nants (called CC&Rs).
- Hedges and trees that grow on lot boundaries are also regulated.
- In some areas, it's customary for neighbors to share the cost of main-taining the fence; in other areas it isn't. It's always a good idea to work with a neighbor and get their input when considering putting up a fence or renovating an old one.

If you're thinking of putting up a fence or a boundary hedge, look first at what's popular in your area. For example, you may love cedar fences but if everyone else has installed vinyl, you may want to follow the crowd. The value of your home also comes from neighborhood appeal. A neighborhood with a mix of fence styles, colors, and upkeep isn't as attractive on one that ties to-gether attractively.

Also, older fences that are eyesores can be stained or painted, and rotting posts and broken slats can be replaced or even shortened to make them attrac-tive again. It's amazing what stain or paint and a little imagination can do in restoring a wood fence.

Hedges are often attractive, but they must be trimmed often and neatly or they quickly become an eyesore that can significantly detract from a home's curb appeal.

In one situation, an investor bought a home for a rental that had a rusty chain link fence along one side, which was an eyesore. Not wanting to dig out the posts, which were set in concrete, the owner planted several Virginia creeper vines along the fence and let nature take its course. Within a year the vines had covered the fence and transformed it into an attractive hedge. Vines, ivy, and other creeping plants can make great cover-ups for eyesores.

Table 6-1 is a roundup of curb appeal killers and pet peeves gleaned from Realtors and appraisers, as well as from comments by home buyers.

Table 6-1. The ten biggest curb appeal mistakes homeowners make.

Curb Appeal Problem	Suggested Action
Yard Clutter	Don't leave hoses, toys, tools, or yard equipment lay about the yard. Invest in a shed to store these items. Most Realtors and buyers agree that the garage is not a good storage area for these items.
Small Items That Really Count	Mail boxes, house numbers, porch lights, and door knockers or bells are important to curb appeal. Visitors and home buyer will notice a banged-up mailbox or a doorbell handing by its wires. Make a to-do list and tackle it.
Bad Driveways	Appraisers knock down value, Realtors hesitate to show, and friends notice and wonder when you're going to fix it. The longer it goes the more it's going to cost you. This should be a top priority before the big screen TV.
Lawn in Poor Condition	The neighbors notice and hope you'll solve it because it affects the neighborhood. A local nursery can advise you on how to solve most lawn problems.
Runaway Landscaping	Appraisers and Realtors find this to be a real problem. It not only lowers value, but makes a home harder to sell. A couple of weekends and sharp cutting tools will do wonders. Neighbors will appreciate it too.
Peeling Paint	This too is a problem that gets more expensive the longer it goes. Failed paint lets water infiltrate, causing more damage to the house, fences, and other wood surfaces. Paint as soon as possible.
Trees Obscuring Home	A very common mistake. When you plant a tree, plan for the size it will be, not what it is now. Trees should frame a home, not tower in front hiding the home.
Fences in Bad Condition	Fences are an important part of curb appeal. Peeling paint, broken or missing slats, and rotting posts need to be fixed and replaced.
Landscaping Not Graded	This an important area with appraisers and home inspectors. Improper grading will channel water to the foundation, and that's not good. Consult a landscaping professional if needed. This problem can lower a home's value big time.
Walks, Decks, and Porches in Bad Condition	These can hold up an appraisal, result in a bad inspection report, and cause buyers to walk away from making an offer. It's also a safety issue if a visitor is injured. Patch or redo as per suggestions in this chapter.

CHAPTER 7

HIRING AND WORKING WITH CONTRACTORS

Few things cause homeowners more frustration, headaches, and money than dealing with contractors, subcontractors (called subs), and small job handymen. Horror stories of botched jobs and misunderstandings abound. But, interestingly, they're mostly the result of communication failures on both sides and of homeowners having unrealistic expectations.

Even top-notch builders face the same homeowner frustrations as the rest of us. Yes, they have dripping faucets and cracked driveways too, but pulling a plumber off the job that's a week behind to fix their problem isn't going to happen. They know they have to deal with their client's problems first.

The gritty truth is that no homeowner has the skills or time to fix or replace all the home's components that fail or wear out. So we must rely on skilled (we hope) tradesmen to come to the rescue. How to find and work with these contractors, subs, and handymen is the focus of this chapter.

If the thought of dealing with a contractor intimidates or leaves you in a cold sweat, you've come to the right place. The following pages will show you how the entire process can be made much easier and save you a lot of money. Some of the things you'll find exciting are:

✓ Tips on how to find a contractor or tradesman

✓ What questions you should ask

✓ How to pay contractors and control costs

✓ How to fire a contractor who isn't performing

✓ The ten biggest mistakes homeowners make and how to avoid them

HOW TO SHOP FOR A CONTRACTOR OR TRADESMAN

Your first step is to find out whether the contractor is experienced and licensed in the type of work you want done. Every state has different licensing requirements. To find out what your state requirements are, go to www.contractors license.org and click on your state. If you have a specific contractor in mind, there's a link to verify that the person is qualified and licensed in your state. Three reasons why you don't want to shortcut this step are:

1. Obviously, you don't want someone who isn't experienced doing the work you want done. Some apprentices may tell you they're masters or journeymen, when they're not.
2. Contractors who are licensed will want to protect their license status and are less likely to skip out on a job.
3. Making sure the contractor is bonded and insured guarantees that if they or one of their employees are injured on the job you won't get a hefty bill or lawsuit.

Your second step is to build a list of possible contractors to contact. Some sources of referrals are:

• Friends, neighbors, and coworkers can be a good resource if you ask them for names of contractors they've used and had good experiences with.

• Architects, mortgage lenders, Realtors, title people, and building supply or home centers can also point you in the right direction.

• Local building associations can sometimes offer a list of members in good standing.

WEBSITES FOR MORE TIPS ON FINDING A CONTRACTOR

www.ftc.gov/bcp/conline/pubs/services/homeimpv.htm
www.hiringacontractor.com/en/default.asp
www.naturalhandyman.com/iip/infcontractor/infhiringcontr.shtm
www.bbb.org/alerts/article.asp?ID = 223
www.oldhouseweb.com/stories/how-to/hiring_a_contractor

When Ron and Teri decided to add on to their home, a 1980s Ranch, and create a master suite with a nursery by bumping out a wall, they hired an architect to work with them. It would cost more (about 15 percent) but they wanted the addition to blend in with the rest of the home and not look like a tacky add-on.

These homeowners felt that the extra cost of having professional help in the design and building of their addition would more than add to the homes value. Other similar homes in their area had been upgraded or added on to, and recent sales showed that they could expect almost a 100 percent return if down the road they decided to sell.

With plans in hand and a rough idea of what it would cost, Ron and Teri's next step was to find a contractor to make their dream happen. They started out with two referrals from their architect and added another from a neighbor who had recently added on to her home. Over the following week they collected five more names from friends, contractor signs on job sites in the area, and one from a local cable TV ad.

This gave Ron and Teri eight contacts on their short list to call and try and set up appointments. The next week was frustrating. Out of the eight, two had declined to bid saying they were too busy with current jobs. Three more said they were interested but it would be five to seven months before they could take on new jobs. That left three who agreed to drop by and take a look at the job and work up bids.

Of course before these interviews took place, Ron and Teri had to:

1. Check with their state contractor's license bureau or city building department websites, or call to verify that the contractor's license was active and in good standing.
2. Check with their state consumer protection agency or local Better Business Bureau to see whether any complaints had been filed. One complaint may not be a problem, but several would eliminate that contractor from consideration.
3. Verify that the contractors were bonded and insured.

As Ron and Teri learned, you may find that getting to that short list isn't going to be easy and may take persistence. The best contractors are busy and may not even return your call or may decline to talk to you about your project.

> **CONSUMER FYI**
>
> The best contractors and trades people usually have all the work they can handle. They don't have to go door-to-door to find business. Plus, when they do a job they seldom have material left over. Sloppy estimating is a fast track to going broke. So when someone knocks at your door and says they'll give you a good deal because they have material left over from a job nearby, don't fall for it.

You can sometimes gain a few points by telling contractors up front who recommended them. Many business people are more responsive if they were recommended by a past client or by someone whom they know.

It's a truism that the best contactors work mostly on referral; word of good work travels fast and it's not long until you'll have to stand in line for their services. Even so, it's sometimes hard to identify the right tradesman for your job, but you can narrow down the odds in your favor by doing your homework.

Once you've got several contractors lined up who have agreed to take a look at your project and give you bid, set up a time to meet with each one.

Plan to have extra sets of plans, specs, photos, drawings, and anything else you can give the contractors to use in working up a bid. You won't make a decision at this meeting: That won't happen until you've gone over your notes, talked it over with your partner, listened to your gut feelings, and looked over the bids when the contractors get back to you.

QUESTIONS TO ASK DURING YOUR INTERVIEWS

Don't hesitate to ask about anything you don't understand, especially about terms and builder jargon. Remember, the only stupid question is the one you didn't ask. The following are some important questions you want answered up front, so be prepared to take lots of notes:

1. Ask how many years they have owned the business? Contractors have a high failure rate the first several years, and it's a good sign if they have survived and prospered more than five years.

2. Ask for a copy of their construction contract. A well-written and professional contract is a big plus. However, you may still want to have an attorney look it over (there are attorneys who specialize in construction contracts), especially if it's a big job.

3. Ask for details of their insurance coverage. Ask to see proof of workers' compensation coverage, liability, and umbrella policies.

4. Ask each contractor to take you to see or set up a time for you to see a couple of completed jobs similar to yours. The relationship between the contractor and past clients is good indication of how the job went. If the job is currently ongoing, notice how the living conditions for the owners are maintained. Are they able to live there as comfortably as possible?

5. Get a list of the past five to ten jobs, along with the home owners' names, addresses, phone numbers, or e-mail addresses.

After you've talked to the three contractors on your short list, the next step is call several of their past clients and see what their experiences were. And no, these past clients won't be offended when you call or e-mail them. Most people are flattered when others seek out their opinions and they have a chance to help out a fellow homeowner. The most common result is that you won't be able to get off the phone, and some will even invite you to look at their remodel.

To make it easier for you, here's a list of questions you can choose from (pick out those that you feel comfortable with) to ask when you call a contractor's past clients:

- Did you enjoy working with _____?
- What did you like best about working with _____?
- Did the job turn out as you envisioned?
- Were they consistent and on time?
- Did they return telephone calls promptly?
- Did you have any changes, and if so, how well did the contractor handle them?
- Did the project start and finish as promised?
- Are there any unresolved issues?
- Would you hire them again for another project?
- Would it be possible for me to take a quick look at your remodel?

Granted, going this route does take some time, but then ask yourself: *What's the alternative?*

After Ron and Teri went through the interview process and called over a dozen people referred by the three builders and visited several past jobsites, a pattern started to emerge.

The contractor who advertised on local cable TV got the job done, but he wasn't consistent and sometimes pulled workers off the job to meet deadlines elsewhere. The contractor referred by a neighbor also did a good job, finished on time and budget, and his past clients were happy with their experience. The third contractor, referred by Ron and Teri's architect, also had happy past customers, although he tended to recommend changes that upped the total cost.

DECIDING ON WHICH BID TO ACCEPT

You may think that choosing among competing bids is going to be like computing a moon-shot trajectory, but in reality they are seldom grouped that close. Here are three tips that'll help you through the process:

• Low bids are not likely to be top quality or the best choice. Perhaps the estimator missed something, or the contractor will end up coming back for more money to complete the project. Be suspicious of any bids that are substantially lower than the rest.

• The highest bid isn't a guarantee of good work or the best choice either. Some builders submit high bids when they don't want the job; it's a good way to say no without offending anyone.

• Most often bids in the middle are more realistic and the ones you should focus on.

In Ron and Teri's remodel, the three contractors got back to them within a week with their bids. The first contractor's bid (the one who advertised on local cable) was lowest at $86,747. The second bid, from the neighbor's referral, came in at $97,453. The third bid was $110,500.

It appeared that the architect's referral wasn't serious about getting the job, and the lowest bid left the homeowners uncomfortable, especially when a couple of past clients complained of inconsistent work flow. Ron and Teri decided the $97,453 bid from the contractor who did their neighbors remodel was the one they would seriously consider.

GOOD PAPERWORK IS CRITICAL

The next step before making a commitment is to look over the contractor's contract. Putting everything is writing is so critical that you should chisel the following on a granite tablet:

If it isn't in writing, it doesn't exist.

That means that all extensions, change orders, and new agreements should be written on addendums, signed by both parties, dated, and numbered 1 of X.

A good contract spells out everything clearly and should include the following:

• Timing—how long the job will take. You should have starting and ending dates clearly spelled out. Also, find out whether the contractor is working on multiple projects and will use unfamiliar subs on your job.

• Who gets the building permits and pays the fees? Usually the builder takes out the permits and you reimburse the fees, or they can be part of the bid.

• Who will supervise the subs, handle problems, and be boots-on-the-project to make sure everyone is on the same page?

• If you're using an architect, has the contractor worked with that person before? A good relationship is important to a smooth job.

• You should have a paragraph spelling out how the contractor will protect the home from construction dust and debris, such as using 6-mil plastic sheeting or tarps supported by a framework enclosing the work area.

• Change orders are a biggie. What happens if you see something that looked great on paper but doesn't look great as the project takes shape?

• Does the builder have a workmanship guarantee and for how long is it valid? What does it cover, specifically?

• What happens if there are misunderstandings. Does the paperwork have a provision for binding arbitration.

• Are the work and materials spelled out in detail. For example, never go with a contract that simply says: "Tear out old deck, dispose of debris, and build new 12 foot by 14 foot deck." It's much better to be specific:

Remove old deck, dispose of debris, install new footings, posts and handrails. Decking to be 2″ × 6″ cedar, custom knotty grade, and fin-

ished with two coats of Sherwin Williams DeckScapes semi-transparent, medium-oak stain. Work and materials to be in compliance with all local building codes.

• How the money is to be paid is, of course, important. There's usually a deposit that shouldn't be more than 10 percent to seal the deal and get the ball rolling. Plan on three to six payments payable as project benchmarks are completed, with the last 15 percent due upon your approval of the job. All payments should be by check or credit card; never, never pay with cash.

• A critical part is proof that the contractor has in force personal liability, worker's compensation, and property-damage policies. Copies of the coverage certificates should be attached to the paperwork.

• You should also have a waiver that frees you from responsibility for litigation or judgments arising from the project. This is important to keep you protected from liability arising from on-the-job injuries and subcontractors' liens (in many states if the contractor doesn't pay his subs, they can place a lien on the property).

MORE INFORMATION ON CONTRACTS

www.b4ubuild.com/resources/contract/index.shtml
www.njsbf.org/njsbf/publications/construction.cfm#2
www.soundhome.com/topics/topic_badcontracts.shtml
www.getvendors.com/household/Residential-Contractor.htm

PAYING THE CONTRACTOR AND MANAGING COSTS

It's not always easy handling the money side of your project. Both you and the contractor are probably wary of getting burned, so it's important to work out a payment plan you're both happy with.

One option is called a *cost-plus*, or time-and-materials, contract, It specifies that you pay for all materials and the contractors are paid an hourly fee in addition to 15 to 35 percent markup for the contractor's overhead and profit.

The final bill would list hours worked as well as paid material invoices from all the suppliers. This is good for the contractors because they're guaranteed to make a profit, which is built into the paperwork. You tend to get good work this way, but costs can easily escalate over budget.

From your end, the biggest downside is that you don't have control over the quality of materials or the costs. To make this arrangement work best, you would need to track all the bills and stay on top of the project to make sure the contractor is working efficiently. There's no real incentive for the contractor to save money.

CONSUMER FYI

If a contractor asks you to pay for a job up front and in cash, you're being scammed. Some states regulate how much deposit a contractor can request. If your state doesn't, never go more than 10 to 30 percent. You may need to go the higher amount if expensive custom materials need to be ordered.

In reality, cost-plus works best for small or handyman type jobs that run a few thousand dollars at most.

Another alternative is the *fixed-fee* contract. With this arrangement, there are usually no surprises at the end. There's usually a mutually agreed-upon allowance for unforeseen changes—$1,000, for example—and everything over this amount you pay for at the time of change. In new construction, these are called *change orders*, and the clients typically pay for these up front or before the change order is completed.

From the contractor's side, if the job is completed for less than bid, the profit goes up. On the flip side, unforeseen problems or sloppy bid-work may result in the contractor losing money.

For the homeowner the pluses are that you know what the costs are and that changes or additions are handled up front for a known cost. The biggest downside is when the contractor underbids or runs into problems, he may cut corners or rush the project to avoid losing money.

As you might expect, this is one reason why you should be wary of bids that come in significantly lower than the others.

Hybrid contracts that combine features from cost-plus and fixed-fee payment plans are sometimes called a *capped cost-plus,* with or without a split. For example, you can add a cap to a cost-plus contract. This option is a time-and-materials agreement with a guaranteed maximum price. If costs stay under the max, the homeowner saves money; if the costs run over, the contractor pays the difference.

The downside to this type of hybrid is that the homeowner gets the savings, which means the contractor has no incentive to cut costs. However, you can create an incentive by giving the contractor 35 to 50 percent of any savings. In reality, this gives both sides an incentive to keep costs down, and in the final tally the homeowner would not be likely to lose any money but could end up with a better job. However, it does entail a higher level of involvement on the homeowner's part. This is not an arrangement where you give the contractor the keys and go off on vacation for a month.

ADDING SWEAT EQUITY TO THE PROJECT

If you have the skills and time you can save some money by doing demo, painting, or sheetrocking yourself. The contractor probably won't go along with you doing code work, such as electrical, plumbing, or roofing; his license is on the line and if you screw up it can cause problems. However, the grunt work is a good pace to save a few bucks.

You'll need to negotiate with the contractor up front exactly what work you'll do. This should be listed specifically on an addendum attached to the construction contract so there'll be no dispute as the project progresses about who does what.

The best time to talk to the contractor about sweat equity is during the bid meeting. Have him work up two bids, one with your participation and the other without it. One contractor who receives many requests from clients wanting to add their sweat equity, says most end up backing out when they look at the bids and realize the time and commitment needed. Still, if you're committed and have the time, you may be able to save up to 25 percent of the total cost, depending on the project and your skills.

> **INTERESTING SWEAT-EQUITY WEBSITES**
>
> www.doityourself.com/stry/sweatequity
> www.askthebuilder.com/017_Homeowner_Sweat_Equity_Jobs.shtml
> www.ezinearticles.com/?FSBO-Sweat-Equity&tid = 390433
> www.make-my-own-house.com/index.htmlaltytimes.com/rtcpages/
>   20060403_sweatequity.htm

Supplying materials may seem like another good idea to shave off a few bucks, but in reality this rarely saves money and can be counterproductive. It's important that the materials and fixtures fit and install as planned. The contractor is responsible, but he can't warrant whatever you supply. Buying fixtures at close-out sales or at a demo yard isn't always the best way to go.

You may also be tempted to talking the contractor into hiring your out-of-work sheetrocker brother-in-law. But the contractor is likely to nix that idea; not because he doesn't like your brother-in-law, but he doesn't know his work. Most contractors use only subs and suppliers they know. That not only makes the work go smoother, but it lowers their liability and possibly yours.

TIPS THAT MAKE YOUR PROJECT GO SMOOTHER

Because you're paying the contractor a lot of money, you want the job to go as smoothly as possible without a lot of additional costs. But all too often homeowners are their own worst enemies. The following six tips will help you keep the work going smoothly:

1.   Never approve details you don't understand or are fuzzy on. Sometimes it's difficult to visualize what a home addition looks like from the blueprints, so keep asking questions until you can picture it clearly. The last thing a contractor wants is clients who panic because what they see isn't what they want. If you have a problem visualizing a project, contact the architectural department of a local university and hire a student to build a model from the plans. This is much cheaper than being unhappy with a remodeling job. Also, a good computer program that gives you 3-D views is available at www.punch software.com/index.htm.

2.   Don't continually change your mind. If you present a moving target to your contractor, you may well end up with a prolonged and way-over-budget project. Do all the necessary planning and shopping for fixtures and materials before the job starts, not afterwards. Keep in mind that change orders are a contractor's profit center and your cost-overrun.

3.   Respect the chain of command. If you need to change or add something to the project, go to the contractor. Trying to work through a tradesperson or sub can come back to bite you. If a problem arises, the contractor may not warrant it. Remember, all changes need to be in writing.

4.   Have a regularly scheduled meeting with the contractor. Depending on the complexity and size of the job, you may want to have brief meeting at the end of each day, or a weekly update. It's important for you to stay on top of what's happening along the way so you won't have surprises at the end.

5.   One thing you want to avoid is letting a disagreement become confrontational. You may have to go the extra mile to maintain your cool, but it's worth it. That a roofer accidentally drops tar on your new Lexus is not license to throw a tantrum. True, you need to be firm and make sure the contractor

keeps his promises as per the contract, but letting a disagreement dissolve into a confrontation can sabotage your project.

6. Once you've hired a contractor, don't second-guess your decision by asking third parties their opinion of the job. Many times there's more than one way to do a job, and getting conflicting opinions muddies up the water and your project. Stay the path you've committed to unless there's good reason believe a problem exists. Good communication between you and your contractor is key to dispelling unwarranted misgivings.

WRAPPING IT UP WITH A WALK-THROUGH AND A PUNCH LIST

No matter how smooth the project's first 95 percent goes, it's the last 5 percent that carries the most emotional weight. Likely, the contractor is in the process of moving on to the next job, and you just want it wrapped up so you can live in a construction-free home.

The key to the final phase is to schedule a walk-through with the contractor so you can work up a punch list. A *punch list* is a list of things that need to be done to finish the job before you sign off on that final 10 or 15 percent of bid amount.

> ### MORE INFORMATION ON PUNCH LISTS
>
> www.servicemagic.com/article.show.Punch-List.13261.html
> www.remodeling.hw.net/industry-news.asp?sectionID = 302&
>   articleID = 211757
> www.ownerbuilder.com/punch-list.shtml
> www.soundhome.com/topics/topic_building.shtml

If you've stayed on top of the project and solved problems along the way, the punch list should be short, and the problems should be quickly taken care of.

A long messy punch list is often the result of not reviewing each day's work, not communicating regularly with the contractor, or letting problems slide until the end. Certainly, you don't want to be a pest on the job, but a quick inspection with the contractor at the end of each day or phase yields big dividends at the end.

However, before you do that walk-through you need to do some homework:

- Before the meeting, review your contract and blueprints and make sure you have copies of all change orders. Create a simple checklist to make sure all the change orders have been completed.
- Walk through the jobsite and jot down anything that needs to be completed, any problems, and any questions that you have.
- Look closely at the finished work. If it's done to your satisfaction and looks good, it probably is. Good finish work is usually the trademark of a good contractor. If you don't trust your judgment, you can hire a professional home inspector to walk through with you.
- Other items to check out are: kitchen backsplash to counter fit, painting dings, trim around doors and windows, counter-tops, and appliances.
- Are the premises left clean and construction debris hauled off?
- Make sure you have a least a half of gallon of paint left for future touch up.
- If there's been an electrical upgrade, have the circuits labeled so you know what the breakers control.

When you meet with the contractor and have done your homework, the punch list walk-through should go quickly. You'll probably find a few minor things that need fixing, which can be done in a day or two. But suppose it's more serious and you find quite a few problems that aren't so minor. In that case, keep the 10 to 15 percent of the bid amount in your checking account until the punch list is completed to your satisfaction.

Suppose everything checks out except for a cabinet that was damaged during installation? In this case you might want to hold out twice the cost of the cabinet and installation. This gives the contractor incentive to follow through or you enough funds to have it done by someone else.

Once the job is complete, you need to create an organized file for all the paperwork. You'll need it when you sell the property, for tax filings, insurance claims or policies, appraisals, and so on.

WHAT IF YOU HAVE TO FIRE YOUR CONTRACTOR?

Antonio and Jennifer hired a local contractor to enlarge the kitchen and create a family room add-on to their 1980s bi-level. They picked this contractor because they liked him and thought he would do a good job, and because the references he supplied said that he did good work. Feeling that they had done adequate homework and eager to get started, they signed a contract. They planned to have everyone over for Jennifer's parents' anniversary in six weeks.

The rough framing appeared to go smoothly and the roof addition and siding blended with the rest of the home. However, once the work moved to the inside, things quickly fell apart. Interior walls weren't straight and the city's building inspector failed the rough plumbing and electrical upgrade.

The homeowners tried to pin down why they were having problems, but the contractor was defensive and blamed it on his subs, who appeared to be cheap labor hired at a local home improvement parking lot.

The pace also slowed down to a crawl: the week without a kitchen, as promised by the contractor, turned into five weeks of take-out and sandwiches. Finally, Antonio and Jennifer reached the breaking point and told the contractor that he was finished and to leave the premises and not return. They next contacted their attorney and asked him to file suit.

Eventually, the homeowners found out the contractor was not licensed in their state and had no assets they could go after. A short time later he disappeared with $6,000 of their deposit, leaving a stack of bills from suppliers for materials not yet paid for.

INTERESTING FIRE-YOUR-CONTRACTOR WEBSITES

www.doityourself.com/stry/contractorfireh2
http://ths.gardenweb.com/forums/load/remodel/msg0921272327406.html?8
www.contractorsfromhell.com

Unfortunate as these situations are, they can often be prevented by following the guidelines in this chapter and by doing your homework.

When you reach that stage, your first option is try to work with your contractor. Perhaps arbitration or a neutral third party can help. Changing builders in the middle of the project is expensive and disruptive. But if all else fails and you need to replace your contractor, your first step is talk to an attorney. You are, in fact, breaking a contract, which can expose you to legal liabilities. If you've been paying only for work done, you're ahead in that the contractor can't disappear with your funds.

However, if it does come to replacing the contractor consider the following:

• Even though the work a contractor does has been unsatisfactory, a lawsuit can tie up the contract amount in escrow, and the job could sit in limbo for longer than you want to live with.

• Try arbitration first, and if that doesn't work, seek for a written termination and full-release agreement with the help of your attorney.

• Make a formal complaint to your state licensing board or local building department. This can sometimes give you some leverage if the contractor faces action from them as well. Some states also have funds that cover losses suffered by homeowners due to wayward contractors.

Finding a replacement contractor presents a whole new set of challenges. Finding a top-notch contractor to take on a botched job isn't going to be easy, and the costs are likely to go up.

First, contractors are going to be wary of the job and of you. They're going to wonder whether you're the client from hell, and they're fully aware that it's expensive to fix someone's else's mess. Plus, they can't predict what it will take to correct the problems, so you may have work on a cost-plus basis.

Still, it's not impossible to find a competent contractor to work with you. Here are some ideas:

• Tell your story, but stick to the facts. Don't rant and rave about how bad the previous contractor was. Stay calm, professional, and focused on the work that needs to be done. Also, make available any paperwork that can help the new contractor access the situation.

• Work up a list of what needs to be done before you solicit bids. You may want to hire an architect, home inspector, or engineer to help you put the list together.

• It's likely that contractors will want to work on a time-and-material basis because of the unknowns, but that leaves you with blue sky over what your projects is ultimately going to cost you. A possible alternative would be split up the project, with payment on an hourly basis for the part that's uncertain and a fixed price for the remainder.

• Learn from your mistakes: Don't shortcut the hiring process discussed earlier in the chapter and make sure the contract has a good termination clause.

HOW TO BE A SMART BUYER OF HOME IMPROVEMENT SERVICES

The first step in becoming adept at hiring home improvement services is to educate yourself on material, products, and how building components are put together. Good sources are magazines, books, home shows, TV programs, and new subdivisions where you can see craftspeople at work. The more you know about what you're hiring people to do, the better job you'll do.

As discussed earlier, it's important to do your homework when picking a contractor. If you find the right contractor, he will supply the subs for the different job components. This makes the project go smoother, but it will be more expensive.

WEBSITES FOR FINDING AND HIRING TRADESPEOPLE

www.mastertrade.co.nz/MAG_WIRED/index.php?edition = 6&article = 84

www.money.scotsman.com/scotsman/articles/articledisplay.jsp?section = Home&article_id = 2444202

www.tradesecrets.org/forms_publications/other_resources/pdf/ hire_certified_tradespeople.pdf

www.realsimple.com/realsimple/gallery/0,21863,1569249,00.html

www.sfgate.com/cgi-bin/ article.cgi?f = /c/a/2003/11/22/ HO15941.DTl

---

Suppose you want to hire people to do certain jobs without going through a contractor or large remodeling company? Sometimes this is a good way to go; other times it isn't. But there's a hard and fast rule you should never break, and that's to match the craftsperson to the job. For example, building a deck and adding a wing to your home takes two different levels of expertise.

This is one of the mistakes Lee and Sherri made when they hired their contractor. He had done decks and small remodeling jobs, but had never tackled a large home addition. When the homeowners called a few of the contractor's references they didn't ask whether the project was an addition; they simply asked whether he had done a good job and got it done on time.

The bottom line is this: If you want to save bucks and hire tradespeople to do specific jobs, you need to do the following homework:

•   What is the total job you want to do?. If it's a remodel or addition that will require several different trades, you may want to consider a general contractor who can pull everything together and coordinate it, like the conductor of a symphony. A single trade job, such as roofing, windows, or plumbing is another matter. That you can usually handle directly.

•   How much of your living space will be affected by the project? If it's considerable, you may want go with a big company that has the resources to put a lot people on the job to get it done faster so you won't miss the Super Bowl.

• How complex is the job? Do you need a specialized company that handles your type of project, such as when repairing fire or flood damage? Specialized remodeling often requires several different trades, and you may be better off going with a contractor with a track record rather trying to hire out the work piecemeal.

• What's the time frame in which you need to job done? If you're not in a rush, a small company may work out. But if you need the job done fast, a larger company usually has more clout with subs and suppliers.

You need to look at the trade-offs: A small one- or two-person company, where you're working with the owner, can give you great customer service and good value. The flip side is that if you need deep pockets, greater breadth of experience, and more resources, then a larger company is a better choice, although it will probably cost more.

PICKING A PRO FOR EMERGENCIES

There comes a time when we all need a pro wearing a tool belt. These are people who practice a single trade, have experience, and have seen about everything in their trade—and that's exactly what we want when water is gushing or an electrical outlet is sparking.

Every homeowner should develop relationships with three trades: a plumber, an electrician, and an HVAC (heating, ventilation, and air-conditioning) contractor before a panic situation arises. The benefits of doing this are many. For example, an HVAC contractor who is familiar with your heating system can respond quickly and know what parts are likely needed. And it's no secret that a call from a familiar customer will take precedence over an unknown call-in.

Finding these trusted tradespeople takes some trial and error. You can minimize the frustration by looking in the right places. Some suggestions are:

• Word-of-mouth is still the best way to find the top performers. Collect a list of names from friends and coworkers to start with.
• Get references from other trades people. For example, plumbers sometimes need electricians when they do a job. Ask the pros for names of other good pros.

- Contractors will sometimes give you names of subs they use. It's in their best interest to keep their stable of subs happy in slow times or during the off-season.
- Even when you get a dynamite referral, don't shortcut the check-'em-out procedure. That means checking for current license and insurance coverage.
- Check out a tradesperson with a small job first, such as a toilet leak or running an outlet to the patio. If they do well and you like their work, add them to your speed dial.

Of course it's important to build and maintain a good relationship once you find a tradesperson you can trust who also does good work—a rare combination. Here are seven ways to help you get into their preferred customer database.

1. Treat contractors and their helpers with the respect you would give clients or other professionals.
2. Be courteous to office help or family members who take your panicky call. You want them to go the extra mile getting you the help you need, instead of putting you on hold or losing your sticky note message because you were rude.
3. If a tradesperson gives you his personal cell phone number, don't abuse the trust and bug him with minor stuff, or give it out to other people.
4. Don't make every call an emergency. If a repair can wait, let them pick the time to do the work.
5. Show respect for the tradesperson's time, by making the job site accessible so she can get right to work, especially if you promised you would do that.
6. Pay the bill promptly and you will be on the contractor's short list of good customers. Paying when the work is completed is best, but sometimes the contractor says he will figure it out and bill you later. Don't betray that trust; pay the invoice promptly when it arrives.
7. Don't keep good tradespeople a secret. Refer them to your friends and those who you know will be good clients.

THE TEN BIGGEST MISTAKES

The ten biggest mistakes homeowners make when hiring and working with contractors are these:

1. Hiring a contractor without checking to see if he is actively licensed, bonded, and his insurance coverage is up to date.
2. Not making sure the contractor has the job experience for the project. For example, building dynamite decks doesn't translate into the ability to handle additions or kitchen remodeling.
3. Not having a good contract and failing to put everything in writing. For substantial jobs, letting a construction attorney look over the paperwork is critical.
4. Failing to get change orders in writing and signed by all parties, detailing the material, time frame, and cost.
5. Not having a good termination clause in the contract.
6. Failing to do your homework and know exactly what you want so you don't create chaos with the builder's timetable and go over budget because of change orders.
7. Not having the last 10 to 15 percent due upon final inspection and approval of the project.
8. Trying to get the contractor to use your materials or hire people he is not familiar with, such as pressuring the contractor to use your out-of-work cousin who happens to be an electrician. You're likely to get a chilly response because contractors have their trusted subs, who they know can perform.
9. Asking the contractor or subs to do little jobs not specified in the paperwork. Resist the temptation of asking for "while you're at it can you . . ." additions or changes without consulting with the contractor and doing the necessary change order.
10. Not staying on top of the project and having regularly scheduled meetings with the contractor to catch problems early. Waiting until the end to address problems can create a long punch list and delay closing out the project.

CHAPTER 8

TAX ASPECTS OF OWNING A HOME

It's no great secret that homeowners get some pretty good tax breaks. Your mortgage lender, Realtor, and numerous magazine and newspaper article tout the advantages of owning versus renting.

That the first $500,000 is exempt from capital gains for a couple is an enticing incentive to buy a home, live in it for a few years, and then sell and move up to bigger home. This in part fuels the high demand for houses and homeownership, which is good for the economy.

But there's also a flip side: Now that you own a home, you become subject to a hefty property tax on your home's value. How much depends on the state you live in and it can vary widely. Because this tax depends on the value of your home according the county assessor, you want to make sure your home is not overvalued. If you think it is, then you can protest and present your case.

How these and other taxes affect you as a homeowner is the focus of this chapter, where you'll learn:

✓ All about property taxes and how to protest a tax bill that's too high
✓ How to turn your property into a tax break
✓ All about capital gains taxes that affect owning and selling property

✓   Which improvements are tax deductible and which ones aren't

✓   What tax credits Uncle Sam wants to give you for being energy efficient

PROPERTY TAXES AND HOW TO KEEP FROM PAYING TOO MUCH

When tax payments become part of the house payment, the tendency is mail a check the first of the month and forget about it. As result, it becomes an out-of-sight/out-of-mind situation. But if you pay property taxes separately, you develop a slightly different perspective. You feel the pain of writing a sizable check on or before November 30th every year, and when the assessment goes up, you are strongly motivated to challenge it. And you should, since according to the International Association of Assessing Officers (IAAO) more than half of the homeowners who protest their assessments get a reduction.

It's important for you to check out how your county handles assessments. Not all states and counties have the exact same rules or quirks. For example, some counties keep your assessment the same if a home is rebuilt on the old foundation (which means you can end up paying the older rate for a nearly new home), while others assess homes based on current market worth.

MORE INFORMATION ON UNDERSTANDING PROPERTY TAXES

www.sctax.org/Tax + Information/property/property.htm
www.ntu.org/main
www.csmonitor.com/2004/1203/p01s01-usec.html
www.usatoday.com/news/nation/2006-08-24-states-property-taxes_x.htm
www.law.freeadvice.com/tax_law/property_tax_law

Understanding how property taxes work is fairly straightforward. There are four simplified steps the county goes through to arrive at the amount they bill you for:

Step 1. The assessor's office determines the value of all the properties in the county. They do this by reviewing appraisals, sold records, computer modeling, and building permits. The assessor then adds up all the real estate values in the county to get a grand total.

Step 2. If your county uses the full-value approach, the assessor simply totals up the appraised values. But if the county uses an assessment ratio—say, one-half—then you multiply the total value of all taxable properties by .50.

Step 3. Each year the county comes up with a new tax rate. This is simply the budget for the money the county needs for the coming year divided by total value of all the real estate in the county. If, for example, next year's county budget is $3,806,000 and the total real estate value for the county is $500,800,000, then dividing next year's budget by the total taxable real estate value in the county gives you a tax rate of .0076.

Step 4. In the final step, the county clerk mails out tax notices to the owners of all the property in the county. The amount you owe the tax collector is the tax rate times the assessment of your house. If, using the above example, the tax rate is .0076 and your house is assessed at $300,000, multiplying $300,000 by .0076 equals $2,280, which is your property tax.

If you think your taxes are too high, there are two approaches you can work with to lower them. One, you can go to the county or city budget hearings and challenge how the government spends the money. If enough people get upset a referendum can put a tax cap on the ballot like what happened in California, Texas and other states.

The other approach is make sure your home's assessment is as low as possible. It the tax notice shows a value you think is too high, you can appeal it.

QUICK CHECKLIST FOR EVALUATING YOUR TAX ASSESSMENT

- Make sure you've received all the deductions you're entitled to.
- Check the assessor's math and your home's property description for accuracy.
- Compare your assessment with three to five similar properties.
- Make adjustments between your home and the comparable properties.

If you feel you have a case after doing this homework, make an informal appeal to the assessor.

APPEALING YOUR TAX BILL

Suppose your tax notice values your house at $200,000. You feel that this is high because you had an appraisal when you refinanced two months ago for

$185,000. Then you happen to talk with your neighbor whose home is a bit larger and has a bigger yard and his tax is $200 less than yours. You wonder how that could happen?

Easy. According to Consumer Reports, tax records show an error rate of 40 percent in estimating property taxes. Also, the National Taxpayers Union writes that as many as 60 percent of all homeowners are over-assessed on their home's value. If this is the case, then most likely you're paying more property tax than you should. Unfortunately, to correct this and put some dollars back in your pocket, you have to be proactive and prove to the county that they owe you money.

What Are the Grounds for an Appeal?

First, an assessment appeal is not a complaint about higher taxes. It's an attempt to prove that your property's estimated market value is either inaccurate or unfair. For a successful appeal you'll need to prove at least one of three things:

1. Items that affect value are incorrect on your property record. For instance, you have one bath, not two. You have a carport, not a garage. Your home has 1,600, not 2,000 square feet, and so on. This is an easy one, you just compare the assessor's record to what you've really got and submit proof such as a recent appraisal or photos.

2. You have evidence (comparables) that similar properties have sold for less than the market value of your property.

3. The estimated market value of your property is accurate but inequitable because it is higher than the estimated value of similar properties. If your home is in a subdivision of similar homes and your neighbors' taxes are less, then you have a case for appeal. A title company, county recorder, Realtors, or websites like Zillow.com all can give you data upon which to build a case. When you receive your assessment notice, read it for instructions about deadlines and filing procedures. They vary from state to state. If they're not clear, call the assessor's office for information. A missed deadline or incorrect filing can cause an appeal to be dismissed.

MORE INFORMATION ON APPEALING PROPERTY TAXES

www.money.aol.com/basics/3canvas/_a/taxes-and-the-homeownerprotesting-
    your/2 0050225133909990011
www.firstam.com/list.cfm?id = 5588

www.google.com/search?q = how + to + protest + property + taxes&hl = en&
  lr = & start = 70&sa = N
www/realtytimes.com/rtcpages/19990601_proptax.htm

The first step in an appeal is usually an informal meeting with someone in the assessor's office. (Sometimes this informal review is handled by telephone or mail.) Information on the mechanics and deadlines for setting up an appointment should be included with your assessment notice, along with additional information for the entire appeals process.

Preparing for the Appeal

Find your property identification number on your assessment notice and use this number to get a copy of your property record from the assessor's office or title company.

Next, review the facts on the property record. Is the architectural style correctly stated? If not, a recent photo of your home will help correct the information. Check the living area of your home, lot size, number of bathrooms and bedrooms, garage or finished basement, construction materials, condition, and so on.

Gather as much information as you can on similar properties in your neighborhood. Ask the assessor's office, call your friendly Realtor who sold you the house, or ask someone you know who has access to the MLS. They can print out a list of comparable sold homes in minutes that you can use for ammunition in your appeal.

Compare your home with the assessed values of similar properties and put together a simple chart comparing the homes feature for feature. Some MLS databases can organize the data from comparable homes into columns and make it easier for you to make comparisons. The key is to know what you're talking about and have the proof to back it up.

Next Step: The Meeting

Follow the instructions on your tax notice and make an appointment with the tax assessor. The purpose of this informal review—which is not yet an appeal—is to verify the information on your property record form and make sure you understand how your value was estimated. Also, the meeting is also used to discover whether the value is fair compared with the values of similar properties in your neighborhood, and to find out whether you qualify for any exemptions.

The person conducting the meeting will probably review your property record form with you and along with information you have about comparable properties. At this time you can present the information you've gathered.

You may not get a commitment for a change in value at this meeting, even though you have uncovered an error or the assessment appears to be inequitable. The decision to change a valuation may have to be made by someone else in writing. If so, find out when you can expect a decision.

In the meeting, view the person you're talking to as an ally, not an adversary. If you're calm, polite, and professional they will likely be more helpful and concentrate on giving you the information you need for an appeal, if it comes to that.

It's possible this is as far as you'll have to go if you get a favorable ruling. If not, then you'll have to proceed to the next step, which is a formal appeal.

The Formal Appeal

Residential appeals are often settled at the local level. If you are not satisfied with the results of your informal review, you have several more opportunities. The first level of formal appeal is usually to a local board. Here you'll need to again present your evidence and point out the similarity between your property and the comparables on your list. Include a recent appraisal of your property if you have one. Close by asking the board to reduce your assessment to what you think is fair based on your data.

Remember to keep it focused and professional. The appeal board is interested only in the fairness and accuracy of your assessment. Don't go off on tangents about how your aging mother needs a lifesaving operation or why you think property taxes are too high.

If you disagree with the local board's decision, additional administrative or legal remedies are available that vary from state to state. Information about these are available from your assessor's office.

Beware of Tax Scams

Around tax time, you'll probably get letters offering to reduce your taxes for a percentage of the reduction. Many legitimate companies offer this service. Typically, they'll charge 30-50 percent of the savings. If you don't have time to protest your tax bill yourself, this can be a better way than not protesting at all. As usual, talk to three companies and get bids and references.

However, beware of scammers who charge a fee up front and promise to lower your taxes or get you a rebate. No one can predict whether and what you can save without going through the system. Always be suspicious if there's an up-front fee involved.

FEDERAL TAXES AND DEDUCTIONS

Over the years you own a home, you'll do a lot of improvements, fix-ups, and repairs. Some of these improvements add to your home's tax basis while others may not. See IRS publication 523 for determining your home's tax basis, or go to www.irs.gov.

Usually, items you replace or repair to keep the home in good condition are not considered improvements that add to its value for tax purposes.

Typical improvements that generally increase your home's value or tax basis are listed in Table 8-1.

Examples of repairs that maintain the home in good condition or prolong its life but don't add to its value are:

Table 8-1. Improvements that generally add value to your home.

Additions	Lawn and Grounds	Heating and AC
Bedrooms	Landscaping	Heating system
Baths	Driveway	Central AC
Decks	Walkway	Furnace
Garage	Fences	Duct work
Porch	Retaining wall	Central humidifier
Patio	Sprinkler system	Filter system
Family room	Swimming pool	Efficiency upgrades
Plumbing	**Interior Improvements**	**Insulation**
Septic system	Built-in appliances	Attic
Water heater	Kitchen remodel	Walls and floor
Soft water system	Flooring upgrades	Pipes and ductwork
Filter system	Central vacuum	
	Wiring upgrades	
Other		
New roof		
Storm windows		
New doors		
Security system		

Repainting the home inside and out

Fixing floors

Fixing rain gutters

Repairing leaks

Repairing walls or ceilings

Replacing broken widows

Replacing carpeting

Any normal maintenance items.

Note that replacing windows with ENERGY STAR-certified upgrades may qualify you for a tax credit.

TAX ADVANTAGES OF WORKING AT HOME

Thanks to broadband technology and laptop computers, more people can work at home and leave the commuting to the rest of the world. To make this a more viable working option, Congress passed the Taxpayer Relief Act of 1997, which contained a modification of the IRS definition of principal place of business.

Beginning in 1999, the new rules allow those who don't have offsite office space to deduct the expenses of a home office. Contractors, sales reps, consultants, and other who perform their services outside their office but need a home office can benefit. However, you must use the office exclusively and regularly for business. In addition, if you use part of your home for business, such as storing records, inventory, or samples, you may be entitled to a deduction.

You can also convert an existing structure or build a separate structure that's not attached to your house. Detached garages, carriage houses, sheds, or small barns make great home office conversions.

What You Can Deduct

Depending on the percentage of your home you use for business, you should be able to deduct portions of utility bills, mortgage interest, repairs, depreciation, cost of a second phone line, office equipment, and any other related expenses. You may also be able to depreciate computers, equipment, and office furniture. However, it's important to set aside the area you use for business. You can't put a filing cabinet in the family room that's used for watching TV and call it an office. The area must be used for business only.

If you decide to claim a home-office deduction, you should keep meticulous records of all your expenses and be prepared to back them up if you're asked to by the IRS.

MORE HOME BUSINESS INFORMATION

www.businessweek.com/smallbiz/0001/tx3666150.htm

www.bankrate.com/brm/news/biz/adviser/20020228a.asp

www.homebusinesstaxsavings.com

www.smallbusiness.yahoo.com/r-subCat-m-1-sc-9-getting_started_home_
business-i

www.homebiztools.com/tax-breaks.htm

There's also a downside to creating a home office. If and when you decide to move, you may have spent $20,000 to create a great home office, but chances are you won't be able to add all of that cost to the price of the home.

Before you draw up plans and get bids for that dream home office you saw in a magazine article, do some "what if" thinking. If you turned a bedroom into an office, can it be restored back to a bedroom without too much trouble or expense.

TURNING EXTRA SPACE INTO TAX BREAKS AND INCOME

When Sharee divorced she ended up with the house and a $1,900 mortgage payment. There wasn't a lot of equity, so selling the house was not an option, nor was letting the home go into foreclosure and ruining her credit.

The home had a finished basement with an outside entrance, two bedrooms, a family room, a full bath, and a wet bar. Sharee figured she could easily covert the wet bar into a kitchenette and rent the basement for $800 a month.

Renting extra space in the attic or basement has spread to more affluent urban areas as well as suburban neighborhoods. Empty nesters, one-income families, widows, and widowers often take in tenants to help pay their mortgages.

Others are adding basement or attic apartments when they build a new home. If you're anticipating caring for parents, or for kids who may come home a second time around, consider adding a finished apartment. If that's not feasible now, at least add the electrical and plumbing rough-in. This is a lot cheaper than retrofitting later on.

FIRST, CHECK OUT THE ZONING

Your first move should be a call to the town zoning department. In most subdivisions, zoning laws limit houses to single-family occupancy. That doesn't mean you can't take in a boarder or two, although that may violate local ordinances. If the tenant is a relative you shouldn't have a problem with adding an in-law apartment. Most zoning departments, insurers, and mortgage lenders will go along with that kind of addition.

But if you want to create an apartment and rent to a nonrelative, check the zoning first. If that is prohibited you may be able to get a conditional use permit or variance. This entails going to the zoning department and filling out the paperwork. There may be restrictions on how utilities are set up as well as inspections for building-code compliance. A hearing may also be required to give the neighbors a chance to protest.

True, this is a more expensive and time-consuming way to go, but in the end it'll be worth it. Some homeowners ignore zoning rules because the city or county is lax in enforcement, and they know they can get away with it. They possibly can for awhile, but it usually comes back to haunt them. Administrations change and all properties eventually are put up for sale. If they sell or refinance, a mortgage lender may want to see the permits. Or the insurance company may deny a claim if you've violated the policy terms and your home is a pile of ashes.

Also, if you're buying a home with an apartment, office, or garage that has been added on or remodeled, you'll want to verify that building permits exist and the house is zoning compliant. Otherwise, you can end up with fines and expensive upgrades. You can also get extended title insurance coverage at closing that insures the previous owners have complied with all zoning and building permits.

Brandon and Julie had this problem when they made an offer on a home with a basement apartment in a great neighborhood near a university. The apartment had been rented out for years, and several other homes on the street also had basement apartments. No one questioned whether the area was zoned for a rental. However, when the appraiser checked the zoning she found it was zoned single family and adjusted her appraisal down.

Although the city zoning department said they hadn't and wouldn't enforce the zoning in this case, they still wouldn't approve the house and apartment for duplex zoning.

This created a sticky situation. As a single family house the appraisal came back $12,000 under sales price. The sellers were upset because now the genie was out of the bottle and the home couldn't be sold as a duplex, lowering the value considerably. And no mortgage lender would finance an illegal duplex. The buyers, rather than walking away from the deal, offered to buy at the reduced price. Reluctantly, the sellers accepted.

> **MORE INFORMATION ON RENTING OUT AN APARTMENT**
>
> www.insurance.com/Article.aspx/Protect_Yourself_When_Renting_Your_Home/
> artid/170
> www.homes101.net/home-buying-tips/bt74
> www.secondsuites.info/Upspercent20andpercent20downspercent20ofpercent
> 20renting.htm
> www.archhousing.org/adu2/renting.htmlwww.ezinearticles.com/?cat = real-
> estate:leasing-renting

The bottom line is: Before you buy a house with an apartment or think of adding one to your home, check the zoning and verify what permits are required. It can save you costly tax, insurance, and zoning headaches later on.

TAX CREDITS FOR MAKING YOUR HOME ENERGY EFFICIENT

When shopping for windows, doors, appliances, and other energy-related items, the IRS will give you a tax credit of up to $500 if you buy products with an ENERGY STAR label. This program is good through 2007, but may be extended.

Even if you don't get a tax credit, the energy-efficient products that qualify for the ENERGY STAR label will save you some serious bucks and make you a more responsible homeowner.

The following products qualify as energy-saving products:

- *Windows/Skylights*. These should have double glazing, low-E coating with insulating gas between the panes. Look for the ENERGY STAR label. Possible tax credit of up to $200.

- *Storm Windows*. These should have double weatherstripping, and have a National Fenestration Rating Council (NFRC) label. Up to $200 tax credit.

- *Exterior Doors.* Look for a polyurethane core and fiberglass or metal skin, foam-filled rubber weather stripping. Look for the ENERGY STAR label. Up to $500 tax credit.

- *Storm Doors.* This should have aluminum frame or vinyl skin over a solid wood core and felt weather stripping. Look for the NFRC label. Up to $500 tax credit.

- *Metal Roofing.* This should include snow guards to control excess run-off and a two-year warranty minimum. Look for the ENERGY STAR label. Up to $500 tax credit.

- *Water Heaters.* The tag should disclose an insulation rating of R-25 and an energy factor of 0.80. Up to $300 tax credit.

- *Insulation.* Applies to all types of home insulation. You'll need the manufacturer's efficiency label. Tax credit of up to $500.

With the emphasis on energy-saving products and the increasing cost of heating and cooling, it's important to look at your home's components and consider replacing older items. It's amazing how often the energy savings catch up with the initial cost in only a few years.

MORE INFORMATION ON ENERGY STAR SAVINGS

www.energystar.gov/index.cfm?c = about.ab_index
www.energy.gov/energyefficiency/energystar.htm
www.energytaxincentives.org

Many states and cities are also jumping on the energy-saving bandwagon by offering their own tax credits and incentives. So before you spend, check and see what's available in your area.

KEY FACTS FOR HOMEOWNERS

Here are some factoids that you need to be aware of as homeowner:

- The IRS defines your main home as the one you live in most of the time. It can be a house, houseboat, mobile home, cooperative apartment, or condo.

- You must have lived in the home for at least two of the last five years.
- If you have more than one home, you can exclude gain only on the sale of your main home, the one you live in most of the time.
- *Gain* is defined as the selling price (line 101 on the HUD settlement statement).
- *Amount realized* is the selling price minus the selling expenses.
- *Selling expenses* are commissions, advertising, legal fees, and loan charges paid by you for the seller, such as points or closing costs.
- *Basis* is determined by how you got the home: What did it cost if you bought it, or what is the fair market value if you got it by inheritance or gift?

Adjusted basis can be increases or decreases to your basis depending on what you did to the home or what happened while you owned it. Improvements that have a useful life of more than one year generally increase your basis. Credits for losses, energy-improvement costs, and so on decrease your basis.

Recordkeeping

Of course, keeping records and receipts of your home improvement projects are critical.

What you should keep are:

- Proof of the home's purchase price and related costs. (These are all on the HUD Settlement Statements you signed at closing.)
- Keep a specific file for improvements, additions, and other items that affect your adjusted basis—that is, the items that add value. This file may also come in handy as a selling tool to document the cost of improvements to a buyer.
- Keep the worksheets (found in IRS publication 523) you used to figure adjusted basis when you sell your home.
- Also keep any other worksheets or paperwork related to your previous home's sale for at least three years, or longer if you have postponed gain.
- If you don't live in the home continuously, you need to have proof of the time you did live in it.

Keeping records also saves you money at tax time. For example, one home-buyer bought an older home that needed a lot of major work. His plan was to live in the home, fix it up, and sell it in a couple of years for a substantial profit.

Knowing that keeping careful track of improvements and costs would be important, the owner-remodeler used Quicken, an accounting program that allowed him to keep track of expenses on his laptop. He also set up a simple system that filed basis-allowable receipts in one folder and nonallowable receipts in another, and he went over his system with a certified public accountant to make sure he didn't miss any allowable deductions.

When the homeowner eventually sold his home, he was able to claim the maximum deductions allowed because he maintained accurate records. In this case, it was critical because the home sold for well over the $250,000 exclusion. This meant that a substantial amount of money was exposed to capital gains taxes, and any missed expenses would have cost the owner money.

TAX-INFORMATIVE WEBSITES

www.bankrate.com/brm/itax/news/20030207a1.asp
www.kiplinger.com/features/archives/2005/01/taxguide2.html
www.quickenloans.com/refinance/articles/homeowner_tax_tips.html
www.energystar.gov/index.cfm?c = products.pr_tax_credits
www.realtytimes.com/rtcpages/20061030_taxwriteoffs.htm

It's very important to keep good paperwork on home-related improvements and upgrades. It's amazing how much money people lose because they don't keep records of their improvements.

THE USE TEST FOR PRINCIPAL RESIDENCE

The rules for meeting the use test are extremely liberal. To take the tax exclusion of a principal residence, all you must do is show that you owned and lived in the property as your main home for either 24 full months, or 730 days during the five-year period, which ends on the date of the sale.

Short temporary absences for vacations or other seasonal absences, even if you rent out the property during these times, are counted as periods of use.

If you own a cooperative apartment, you must have owned the stock for at least two years and lived in the apartment for at least two years.

There are exemptions to the above rules if you have to sell because of health, employment, unforeseen circumstances, and so on (see the worksheets in IRS Publication 523).

You may also want to keep your home as an investment, Renting it can be a good strategy when the market is slow and you can't sell the home. For example, Dan and Sheila tried to sell their home of twenty years when he got a better job offer in another state. A few months prior, they had refinanced the home and ended up with a loan that was more than what they were able to sell their home for.

Not wanting to give up his job offer, Dan and Sheila decided to rent their home for a year or two in hope of the market improving to where they could break even. After renting the home for over two years, the local market did go up. They were able not only to sell the home but to walk away with a good profit. Because they had lived in the home two out of the last five years, they were able to sell the home without a taxable gain.

Another way to defer taxable gain is with a 1031 exchange. It's not a way to avoid taxes, but it is a great tool for building equity and transferring it from property to property.

1031 TAX-DEFERRED EXCHANGES

This underutilized financial tool can make a big difference when:

1. You want to keep your starter home for a rental when you move up.
2. You've rented part of your home and it's subject to capital gains.
3. You want to trade your single family up to a duplex or fourplex.
4. Someone has an investment property (single-family rental, duplex, or even a newly built home) you would like, but if they sold, capital gains would kick in.

The possibilities are endless for creating win-win deals and deferring capital gains to a time when the tax bite is not so painful.

Unfortunately, paying capital gains taxes keeps many owners from selling single-family homes and condos that have increased in value past their exemptions. Not wanting to go through the pain of fixing up the property and putting it on the market, many owners continue living with the problem and procrastinating instead of doing something proactive. As equity grows, the problem grows.

Luckily, a 1031 exchange may be able to solve these problems by getting owners into something more suited to their interests.

Putting an exchange together is fairly straightforward, but it may require the expertise of an exchange intermediary, accountant, and a title/escrow company, depending on the number of properties and the complexity involved. The exchange intermediary is the neutral party that handles the nuts and bolds of the exchange. To find one, look in the yellow pages or check the Internet under "real estate exchange." Better still, Realtors and title companies who do 1031 exchanges will be able to recommend good intermediaries. You'll also need a title or escrow company to handle title work and funding.

The exciting thing about 1031 exchanges is you don't have to have two property owners who want to exchange straight across, you can bring in other buyers and sellers with their properties to add to the mix.

Here's a simplified example: You find a buyer for the property you want to get rid of (relinquished property) and the sale goes in escrow. You have forty-five days to find a property you want to buy (replacement property) and that goes into the escrow. The buy/sell mix closes and you end up with the property you want. The party with the least equity can use cash or financing to make up the difference.

Profiting from an Exchange

When Norm and Susan were transferred from Utah to Georgia, they planned on returning in a few years. Therefore, so they rented their home and a smaller property they had bought from an estate. However, five years later Norm and Susan decided to stay in Georgia and sell the homes. Unfortunately, they no longer qualified for owner-occupied status, so they decided to invest in local rental property and defer capital gains taxes.

Their strategy was to put the proceeds from the sales into a 1031 exchange escrow with a title company in Utah and find a rental property in Georgia. When they closed on the property where they lived, the funds would be released from escrow and used for a down payment. The balance of the purchase price would come from a nonowner-occupied mortgage.

Luckily, the tenants in the smaller home wanted to buy it and were able to qualify for the mortgage payments, which were $80 less than their rent payment. The sale closed and the $97,000 proceeds—after paying off a small mortgage and selling costs—went into the title company exchange department's escrow account.

While the paperwork for the rental sale was going forward, Norm and Susan were out looking for rentals in their area. The market was tight and they didn't find anything they liked until two weeks after their home in Utah had closed. (The IRS allows 45 days to identify a property and up to 180 days to close the deal.) They made an offer on a two-bedroom condominium in a good area for $185,000, and it was accepted.

The $97,000 in escrow was used for a 20 percent down payment, and the balance was financed with a nonowner-occupied mortgage. The equity from one rental home in Utah was transferred to Georgia with no capital gains taxes.

Norm and Susan's other rental has six months to go on a lease. If the tenants can't or don't want to buy it, it'll go on the market and the process will be repeated.

As you can see, the 1031 exchange is a great way to transfer equity from one area to another and defer capital gains taxes. If you're in a difficult market, need to move, and can't sell your home, you can rent it until the market improves and still build equity.

Rules for a 1031 Exchange

Here is a quick summary of the rules for a 1031 exchange:

• The IRS requires the exchange to be like-kind, which it identifies as "real estate for real estate." You can exchange a duplex for bare land, office building, warehouse, or whatever. Just as long as it's real estate that is not used as a primary or secondary residence.

• From the date of closing on the sale of the relinquished property, you have 45 days to find the replacement property(s) and 180 days to close.

• You must insert a clause into all sale contracts that identify the transactions as a 1031 exchange. The IRS needs to see an easy-to-follow paper trail.

MORE INFORMATION ON 1031 EXCHANGES

www.irs.gov—download Publication 544, Form 8824.
www.realtor.org/libweb.nsf/pages/fg408
www.homebuying.about.com/cs/1031exchange/a/1031_exchanges.htm
www.homebuying.about.com/od/1031exchange
www.realtyexchangers.com
www.wave.net/immigration/lawyer/tax_avoid.html

John and Angie went the exchange route when they decided they no longer wanted the demands of being a landlord. They owned a duplex that had about $80,000 in equity, and they didn't want to pay out a big part of their equity in taxes. Although they didn't want to exchange for more rental property, undeveloped land appeared to be a good way to go because there is low main-tenance, no rent to collect, and no late-night plumbing problems to fix.

Finding a buyer for their duplex was easy, and the sale closed with the proceeds going into escrow. Their Realtor found a ten-acre parcel for sale that appeared to be in the path of eventual development.

Since the land cost $139,000, John and Angie needed about $59,000 to make a deal. They decided to take out a ten-year, low-interest equity line of credit on their home for the funds needed to complete the deal. The second leg of the 1031 exchange closed and everyone was happy.

As a result of the exchange, a young couple starting out was able to buy a duplex they had been searching for. John and Angie won't have to collect rents or do maintenance on their days off. Everyone wins and the tax man has to wait for another day to collect his due.

In another case, an investor had several rental homes that he and a friend had owned for several years, The values had increased substantially along with the tenant headaches. Wanting to get rid of these headaches and buy some land, they found a ten-acre parcel that had promise of going up in value over the next few years.

The owners made an offer on the land subject to their rental properties selling over the next sixty days. However, the landowner had been thinking the deal over and decided he wanted to be a landlord so he offered to take one of the homes as a part of the deal. That left three homes that needed to be sold and the proceeds escrowed for a 1031 exchange.

Everything went as planned, the threes homes sold and the exchange closed. The former landlords ended up with a parcel of land where the only upkeep was cutting the weeds once a month.

Table 8-2 lists the typical steps involved in making a 1031 tax-deferred exchange.

As you can see, exchanges are a great way of turning a stale real estate investment into something more exciting for all parties with the taxes deferred.

FEDERAL TAX CONSIDERATIONS WHEN SELLING

Currently the tax code allows an individual $250,000 and a married couple filing jointly $500,000 tax-free when selling a principal residence. A few years ago this didn't seem like a big problem in many areas of the country. However, homes prices have escalated to the point that many more homeowners will be going over the limits and end up reporting capital gains on Schedule D (Form 1040).

When you upgrade and improve your home to sell, keep track of what you

Table 8-2. Steps to a 1031 exchange.

Steps	What's Involved
List property for sale and line up a property exchange intermediary. The intermediary can be a title company or an attorney who is experienced in exchanges.	Include a notice in the listing and sales documents that the property is part of a 1031 exchange. As a seller you will assign the role of grantee or transferee of the deed to the intermediary.
A buyer for property is found.	The intermediary prepares an assignment assigning the role of seller to the intermediary along with the other exchange paperwork, which goes to the closing agent
The sale is closed and equity funds are put in escrow.	Exchanger and buyer sign assignment agreement, which assigns intermediary the role of seller in the sale. The 45-day clock starts ticking on identifying an exchange property.
The hunt for a replacement property should be well on its way by this time.	45 days to find property and identify it in writing by street address or legal description. This is faxed to the intermediary.
Exchanger makes an offer on the property.	Included in the purchase agreement is a notice that the deal is part of a 1031 exchange with the required assignments. This usually is not a problem with the sellers, they just want their money and to be on their way.
In case of multiple properties and multiple exchangers:	All the legs of the exchange are put into escrow and closed with each party getting its designated property at the about the same time. Closing and funding has to be within the 180 days.
File tax forms.	Exchangers file Form 8824 with the IRS and file any other state-required forms.

do and keep the receipts. Some of your expenses in showcasing your home may increase your basis and may be a tax break.

Even if you others do your tax return, look over IRS publication 523, *Selling Your Home,* to get an idea of what tax breaks you can take.

Other IRS publications that may affect your tax situation are:

521, Moving Expenses

527, Residential Rental Property

530, Tax Information for First-Time Homeowners

544, Sales and Other Dispositions of Assets

547, Casualties, Disasters, and Thefts

551, Basis of Assets

587, Business Use of Your Home

936, Home Mortgage Interest Deduction

THE FIVE BIGGEST TAX MISTAKES HOMEOWNERS CAN MAKE

1.   Not keeping good records and receipts of upgrades and improvements that affect your home's basis. This is especially critical when your home's value is over $500,000 (for a married couple) and you have capital gains exposure.

2.   Not looking at the property tax statement and checking to make sure you are credited with all the exclusions possible and that the math is correct. Many homeowners whose property taxes are paid by the lender fail to do this. It's an out-of-sight/out-of-mind situation.

3.   Failing to check the property tax assessment against what similar properties are assessed. It's been estimated that nearly 75 percent of homeowners who protest get a reduction. The burden is on you, not the assessor, to make sure you're not overcharged.

4.   Not following through with a protest during the window period (typically three to six weeks). Check your county website for this window period.

5.   Failing to compare your home's assessment on your tax statement to the purchase price. If the assessment is higher, protest and take in your closing documents to verify the selling price.

CHAPTER 9

INSURANCE MATTERS FOR
HOMEOWNERS

For many new homeowners, homeowner's insurance is one of those back-burner items that appeared on the closing statement as just another charge they had to pay. Actually, depending on the area you live in, there were likely several different insurance policies listed in the buyer's column, including homeowner's insurance, flood insurance, private mortgage insurance (PMI), title insurance, homeowner warranties, and sometimes even mortgage life insurance.

Tucked away in the thick folder of closing documents, these policies are largely forgotten until a problem occurs, when suddenly they become very important.

With so many unknowns that can carry a big price tag, homeowner's insurance and some of the other insurance options become an investment, not an expense. Remember that: *It's an investment*.

While insurance can be as boring as watching paint dry, ask homeowners from the Louisiana or Mississippi coasts how they feel about insurance after

Katrina washed away or flooded their homes. Boring, yes—but financially critical to you as a homeowner. In this chapter you'll learn:

✓ All about homeowner's insurance and what it covers

✓ How to shop for a policy and get the best deal

✓ What records you need to keep so you can prove your claim

✓ What other types of insurance you may want to have

✓ All about title insurance and why you need it

WHAT HOMEOWNER'S INSURANCE DOES AND DOES NOT COVER

Carrie found this out what homeowner's insurance covers just one day after closing on an updated bungalow in an upscale but older area. During move in, she turned on the tub and another faucet to flush out the drains but got distracted for a few minutes and let the water run. Later when she went downstairs, she found to her horror a foot of water in the basement. Water had backed up through a floor drain in the laundry and flooded the finished basement.

A plumber checked out the line to the street and found tree roots had invaded the sewer pipe and created a partial obstruction. Normal flow of a toilet or faucet was not a problem, but the line couldn't handle the larger volume when two faucets were opened full.

Although Carrie had a professional inspection of the property before closing, the inspector didn't find any problems because the roots that caused the obstruction came from a tree that had been removed several years earlier. The tree stump had also been removed and grass planted over the area; there was no way to tell a tree once grew there.

The damage to the basement was considerable, with soaked sheetrock, carpets, and some furniture. Luckily, Carrie had a good homeowner's policy that paid for the damage, less her $500 deductible.

A good homeowner's policy protects you from the double whammy of having your home damaged or destroyed and still having a mortgage to pay off. The mortgage people know this and they want to protect their security. That's why many lenders collect one-twelfth of the yearly premium each month with your payment. Each year when the policy comes due the mortgage company pays the bill from the funds collected and held in an escrow account.

INFORMATIVE HOMEOWNER'S INSURANCE WEBSITES

www.iii.org/individuals/homei
www.pueblo.gsa.gov/cic_text/housing/12ways/12ways.htm
www.consumeraction.gov/caw_insurance_homeowner_renter.shtml
www.akc.org/insurance/homeowners_inscenter.cfm
www.insuremyhouse.com
www.iii.org/media/facts/statsbyissue/homeowners

If you have a conventional loan with a down payment of 20 percent or more, you can sometimes handle the insurance on your own. FHA- and VA-insured programs, however, still require the monthly escrow for taxes and insurance on all their programs.

If you're handling it on your own, don't forget to renew your policy. If you let it lapse, your former insurer will notify the mortgage company, and they will cover your home with a single vendor policy. These policies protect the mortgage company's interest only and are expensive, costing you about double what a homeowner's policy would. So don't let your homeowner's lapse. It can be very expensive.

Policy Options

Homeowner's insurance evolved in the late 1950s, when the insurance industry needed a single comprehensive policy to cover not only the house, but the contents and liability. The standard policy has two parts: property insurance and personal liability.

The most common policy, HO-3, covers the house and other structures for everything except floods, earthquakes, and other policy exclusions. This is the policy that most mortgage lenders require you to carry as a loan condition.

Other options are HO-1, a bare-bones policy that is not available in most states, and HO-2, which covers only risks that are specifically insured. HO-4 is designed for renters, and HO-6 covers condominium and co-op owners.

HO-8 is designed for older homes and reimburses you for damage on an actual cash value basis. That means replacement cost minus depreciation. Depending on the area and house, full replacement cost policies may not be available for some older homes. In fact, they are getting harder to find in just about all areas. The different policy options and what each type of policy covers are summarized in Tables 9-1 and 9-2.

Table 9-1. Different types of homeowner policies.

Type of Policy	What It Covers
HO-1	Bare bones police. No longer available in most states.
HO-2 (broad)	Covers most perils. Also a available for mobile homes.
HO-3	The most popular policy. Protects from all perils except those excluded in the fine print. Typical exclusions are floods, earthquakes, war, etc.
HO-4	Renters policy. Protects possessions only against the same perils as HO-3.
HO-6	Homeowner's policy for condo or co-op owners. Covers what you own against the same perils as a HO-3. A master insurance policy covering the structure is included in your Homeowner Association fees.
HO-8	A policy for older homes. Reimburses you for damage on an actual cash value, which means replacement cost minus depreciation. This policy will not usually reimburse you for the costs of bringing a home up to code.

Policy Options to the Above	
Actual Cash Value	Will replace home and possessions minus a deduction for depreciation.
Replacement Cost	Pays the cost of rebuilding/repairing the home or replacing possessions without a deduction for depreciation.
Guaranteed or Extended Replacement Costs	Offers the highest level of protection. Pays whatever it costs to rebuild your home to what it was before the disaster. You may need an Ordinance or Law rider to pay for any costs to bring home components up to code if the home is dated. This policy may not be available for older homes. (Some companies will go only 20–25 percent over the policy limit on this type of coverage.)

STANDARD COVERAGE

The standard policy (HO-3) typically covers damage to both structures and personal property from fire, lightning, windstorms, hurricanes, tornadoes, hail, explosions, aircraft, vehicles, smoke, theft, vandalism, falling objects, damage from ice, snow or sleet and freezing pipes. However, as many homeowners found out after Hurricane Katrina, how insurance companies define flood damage versus other hurricane-related damage can give you problems when you file a claim. Since damage from floods is not covered in homeowners poli-

Table 9-2. What your policy covers and doesn't cover.

Possible Claim	Basic HO-1	Broad HO-2	Special HO-3	Renters HO-4	Condo HO-6	Older home HO-8
Fire or Lightning	YES	YES	YES	YES	YES	YES
Windstorm or Hail	YES	YES	YES	YES	YES	YES
Explosion	YES	YES	YES	YES	YES	YES
Riot or Civil Disturbance	YES	YES	YES	YES	YES	YES
Damage by Aircraft	YES	YES	YES	YES	YES	YES
Damage by Vehicles	YES	YES	YES	YES	YES	YES
Smoke Damage	YES	YES	YES	YES	YES	YES
Vandalism	YES	YES	YES	YES	YES	YES
Theft	YES	YES	YES	YES	YES	YES
Volcanic Eruption	YES	YES	YES	YES	YES	YES
Damage from Ice, Snow, or Sleet	NO	YES	YES	YES	YES	NO
Falling Objects	NO	YES	YES	YES	YES	NO
Interior Water Damage from Household Plumbing, Heating/AC, or Appliances	NO	YES	YES	YES	YES	NO
Freezing of Pipes and Appliances	NO	YES	YES	YES	YES	NO
Electrical Overload Damage to Wiring	NO	YES	YES	YES	YES	NO

Note: Additional and specific perils can be added to your policy, such as coverage for earthquakes, mudslides, or extra valuables.

cies, you need to read the fine print and make sure you understand exactly what isn't covered and add additional coverage if needed.

Personal liability is also covered if you or your property injures someone. Just about everything is covered unless specifically excluded. Typical exclusions are floods, earthquakes, neglect, intentional loss, earth movement, power failure and damage caused by war. Also, if you have a loss and the building codes have changed, increasing the repair or replacement costs, you'll pay the difference.

For example, if you have a fire and your home's electrical system is an older 60-amp-fuse system, you'll end up picking up the cost to upgrade it as well as all other upgrades needed to bring the home into code compliance.

Also, there are limits on the losses that can be claimed for items such as cash, furs, jewelry, or hobby collections. You'll need to decide if you want buy supplemental coverage to increase your protection.

One worthwhile supplemental item is coverage for living expenses if your home is destroyed or damaged and you have to move out for awhile. It covers hotel bills, restaurant meals, and other living expenses incurred while your home is being rebuilt. Coverage for additional living expenses differs from company to company. Many policies provide coverage for about 20 percent of the insurance amount on your house. You can increase this coverage, however, for an additional premium. Some companies sell a policy that provides an un-limited amount of loss-of-use coverage but for a limited time. It doesn't take much damage to a home for you to be glad you added this option to your policy.

In addition to standard coverage, there are three levels of coverage: re-placement, extended, and guaranteed replacement. They differ in the amount of money a claim pays and what is covered. Of course, the better the coverage, the higher the cost of the policy. Highlights of these three coverage levels are:

Replacement Coverage

Most insurance companies offer replacement cost coverage. For an additional 10 percent or so, insurers will pay what it costs to replace your home and belongings up to the amount of your coverage. For example, if your TV set that cost you $700 is damaged in a fire, you'll get the full cost covered. But under standard coverage you would get replacement cost *minus* depreciation. Because the depreciation schedule for electronics is steep, you would be lucky to get 50 percent, or $350, for the TV. Or if your $50,000 tile roof, which is rated for twenty years, is destroyed in a fire when it's only ten years old, you would get only a $25,000 reimbursement under standard or actual cash-value coverage.

Extended Coverage

The next step up in coverage is extended coverage. You insure the home for the appraised value, and the policy will pay up to 125 percent to cover unforeseen problems. Extended coverage gives is the minimum you should carry if you have a high LTV (loan-to-value) mortgage. With standard coverage, a major fire would most likely leave you with an insurance check many thousands of dollars less than your mortgage balance. This is why many mortgage lenders require you to have this higher level of protection, but it will cost you more.

Guaranteed Replacement

But the best protection is guaranteed replacement cost which has no present limit on what it'll take to replace your home and contents. However, because of big losses in recent years, many insurance companies have dropped this policy. You may have to shop around. If you can find it, it's definitely worth considering, especially if you have recently bought your home and don't have much equity.

YOU'LL NEED THIS RIDER IF YOU BUY AN OLDER HOME

Don't assume that if your policy reads "Guaranteed Replacement" that you're fully covered in case of a disaster. The guarantee can mean different things at different companies, but it usually applies if the cost of rebuilding a home is higher than the face value of your policy.

If you buy an older home chances are some of the wiring, plumbing, heating/cooling systems, and structure may no longer meet newer building codes. If you have a fire, the insurer is required to replace what you had, not what you're required to have in order to rebuild.

So here's the catch: When you rebuild you'll need to include the newer building codes and upgrades. That expense isn't included in your policy. And those upgrades can cost you a bundle.

You can solve this potentially expensive problem by getting something called Ordinance and Law coverage. This is a rider to your policy that applies to the costs of upgrading your home to meet existing building codes. However, keep in mind that this rider will pick up the tab only for bringing the damaged part of the house up to code. It will not pay for bringing the undamaged part of structure up to code. In other words, you could be better off if the house were totaled than only partially damaged.

Rick and Andrea had this happen when they bought a 1940s brick bungalow with the dream of restoring it. They loved the wood floors and trim, the brick construction, and the wide front porch.

The home still had the old-style wiring through a fuse box, which should have been the first upgrade project. But Rick and Andrea had decided to start on the floors, wood trim, and interior decorating. Sometime during the second week of restoration, debris got into an electrical receptacle after the faceplate was removed. The old wiring sparked, igniting the partially stripped wallpaper and engulfing the wall in flames. Fortunately, the fire department was nearby and reacted quickly. Only the front part of the house was gutted.

After getting together with the insurance adjuster and their agent, Rick and Andrea were shocked to find out it would cost them over $12,000 out of their pocket to restore the house. Their insurance policy would restore the home to "as was" condition, but not pay to bring it up to code. And they could not get a building permit unless the house incorporated building code upgrades.

So what's the bottom line? If you buy an older home, make sure the home inspector gives you a list of items that don't meet current building codes. Wiring and heating systems are often at the top of the list for potential fires.

As your budget allows, first upgrade those items on the list that don't meet code. By doing this, you'll not only make your home safer, but increase its value. If disaster strikes it will be replaced to "as was" condition and you won't be out the money you spent on improvements.

Also, be sure to keep all the contracts, receipts, and paperwork in a safe place so you can document these improvements. This is where photos or a video can be worth thousands of dollars to you.

THREE COMPONENTS OF A HOMEOWNER'S POLICY

It's important to look at your basic policy components—structure, personal property, and liability—to see if you have enough protection. Even if you don't live on the San Andreas fault or collect antique firearms, you'll probably need to get additional coverage for peace of mind.

> In Texas, policies vary somewhat from those in most other states. Check out www.tdi.state.tx.us for more information.

Structure

Many common problems, such as earthquakes, floods, failed sump pumps, and backed-up sewers, aren't covered in basic policies. To get this additional coverage you'll need to add endorsements or riders. The higher a certain risk is for your area, the more important it is to add this coverage. Coverage for sewer clogs is usually less than $50, but it's a must, especially for older homes. A sewer backup is especially expensive because it takes special cleanup procedures due to contamination.

This is why Carrie had to call in a disaster cleanup company to handle her sewer backup mentioned earlier in the chapter, and it added a couple of thousand dollars to her clean up costs.

Personal Property

All polices include coverage for the contents of your house, but often the amount isn't enough. Basic plans commonly pay 50 to 70 percent of the policy amount. For example, a $175,000 policy would likely give you anywhere from $87,000 to $122,000 for the contents. This may sound like a lot, but when you go through your home and total up everything you've got, it'll be a shock. The value adds up fast when you total furniture, electronics, wardrobes, power tools, stamp collections, and so on.

If you have expensive items, such as gun or art collections, antiques, jewelry, or computer equipment, you may want to consider extra coverage based on their actual value.

Liability

Most policies have $100,000 minimum liability coverage that protects you in case someone is injured on your property. Whether that's enough depends on much you have to lose if someone sues you. You can pay for additional protection, and you can also add an umbrella policy that covers you for incidents away from home.

When you have a home business or office, and you have people coming to your home, your liability can skyrocket. Adding a $1 million umbrella policy for about $200 a year makes good sense.

If you own a condo or co-op, you'll be dealing with two policies. The homeowners association or co-op board will have a master policy that covers the common areas—roof, basement, elevator, boiler, and walkways—for both liability and physical damage. You are responsible for the other policy—the HO-6—that covers your personal possessions, structural improvements to your apartment, and additional living expenses. It also covers you for fire, theft, and the other disasters listed in your policy, as well as provides liability protection.

To adequately insure your apartment, it is important to know what structural parts of your home are covered by the condo/co-op association and what aren't. You can find out by reading your association's bylaws and/or proprietary lease. If you have questions, talk to your association or board as well as to an insurance professional.

Some associations insure the individual condo or co-op units, as they were originally built, including standard fixtures. In that case, the owner is responsible only for alterations to the original structure of the apartment, like remodeling the kitchen or bathtub. Sometimes this includes not only improvements you make, but those made by previous owners.

In other situations, the condo/co-op association is responsible only for insuring the bare walls, floor, and ceiling. The owner must insure kitchen cabinets, built-in appliances, plumbing, wiring, and bathroom fixtures.

Other coverage options you may be able to get, depending on area, association, or board are:

1. *Unit Assessment.* This reimburses you for your share of an assessment charged to all unit owners as a result of a covered loss. For instance, if there were a fire in the lobby, all the unit owners would be charged for the costs of repairing the loss.

2. *Water Back-Up.* This insures your property for damage by the back-up of sewers or drains. Make sure that water back-up is included in the policy.

3. *Umbrella Liability.* This is an inexpensive way to get more liability protection and broader coverage than is included in a standard condo/co-op policy.

4. *Flood or Earthquake.* If you live in an area prone to these disasters, you will need to purchase separate flood and earthquake policies. Both flood and earthquake insurance can be purchased through your insurance agent.

5. *Floater or Endorsement.* If you own expensive jewelry, furs, or collectibles, you might consider getting additional coverage since standard policies generally have a $1,000 to $2,000 limit for theft of jewelry.

When you're buying insurance, it's important to find an agent or company that specializes in condominiums or co-ops. You can reduce your rates by raising your deductibles and by installing a smoke- and fire-alarm system that rings at an outside service. Also don't forget to check on discounts if you insure your unit with the same company that underwrites your building's insurance policy. Shop around and get at least three quotes, because costs can vary considerably.

IMPORTANCE OF A HOME INVENTORY

In case of loss, would you be able to remember all the possessions you've accumulated over the years? Having an up-to-date home inventory will help you get your insurance claim settled faster and verify losses for your income tax return.

> **HOME RECORD-KEEPING WEBSITES**
>
> www.libertystreet.com/asset-home-inventory.htm
> www.iii.org/media/publications/brochures/homeinventory
> www.onlineorganizing.com/usefullinkssubcategory.asp?subcategory=home
>   inventory
> www.pueblo.gsa.gov/cic_text/money/keeprecords/keeprecords.htm
> www.iii.org/individuals/homei

Rocky and Lisa's home was completely destroyed a few days after Christmas. A flue in their wood-burning stove developed a crack that allowed hot gases to ignite a wood beam in the ceiling.

Luckily, they had gotten a video camera for Christmas and decided to tape their house and possessions after reading a magazine article about fire safety. The camera was one of the few items they saved, and the video was still in it along with some now precious family footage.

The videotape saved these homeowners a lot of problems and thousands of dollars. There's no way they could have remembered or proven everything they lost in the fire without it.

The lesson learned here is to keep copies of vital records, pictures, and videos at a safe and/or remote location.

How to Inventory

Start by making a list of your possessions, describing each item and noting where you bought it and its make and model. Add any sales receipts, purchase contracts and appraisals you have. For clothing, count the items you own by category—pants, coats, shoes, for example—making notes about those that are especially valuable. For major appliance and electronic equipment, record the serial numbers usually found on the back or bottom of the item.

If you've just bought a home, work up a list as you are moving in and unpacking. Use the following guidelines:

- Valuable items like jewelry, art work, and collectibles may have increased in value since you received them. Check with your agent to make sure that you have adequate insurance for these items. They may need to be insured separately.

• Take pictures of rooms and important individual items. On the backs of the photos, note what is shown, the make, and where you bought it. Don't forget things that are in closets or drawers.

• Videotape your home. Walk through your house or apartment videotaping and describing the contents. Or do the same thing using a tape recorder.

• Use your PC to make your inventory list. Personal finance software packages often include a homeowner's room-by-room inventory program.

• Regardless of how you create the inventory (written list, CD, photos, videotape, or audio tape), keep it along with receipts in your safe deposit box or at a friend's or relative's home. That way you'll be sure to have something to give your insurance representative if your home is damaged.

HOW TO PICK AN INSURANCE COMPANY

Many homebuyers don't take the time to shop for the best insurance deal. Their mortgage lender calls and tells them they need to have an insurer send a HO-3 binder so the deal can close. Letting the lender choose or asking friends or coworkers who they use is not the best way to find the best insurance deal.

Four things you need to look for when shopping for an insurance company:

1. *Price.* Insurance policies and prices vary greatly from one company to another, so it pays to shop around. Get at least three price quotes from companies, agents, or from the Internet. Check with your state insurance department, because they may publish a guide that shows what insurers charge in the various parts of your state.

2. *Insurer Stability.* Make sure that the company you buy from is financially stable and likely to be around to pay any claims. Few things are more devastating to your financial future than to have your home burn down and then find out that the insurance company can't or won't handle your claim.

3. *Service.* The insurance company and its representatives should answer your questions and handle your claims fairly, efficiently, and quickly. You can get a feel for this by talking to other customers who have used a particular company or agent. Also check with your state insurance department to see whether they have a complaint ratio that compares the number of valid complaints with the company's share of policies in your state.

4. *Availability.* Whether you buy from a local agent, directly from the company by phone, or from the Internet, you should be able to contact the

company or agent easily. If you can't, consider getting another company. Fast and easy claim service is one of the basic things you're paying for.

> **WEBSITES FOR PICKING AN INSURANCE COMPANY**
>
> www.ezinearticles.com/?How-To-Pick-The-Best-Home-Insurance-Company&
>   id = 381585
> www.iii.org/individuals/homei/hbs/pickco
> www.money.aol.com/insurance

Some of the factors an insurance company uses to determine the price of your policy are:

- Your credit rating score.
- The square footage of the house and any additional structures.
- Building costs in your area.
- Your home's construction, materials, and features.
- Amount of crime in your neighborhood.
- The likelihood of damage from natural disasters, such as hurricanes and hail storms.
- The proximity of your home to a fire hydrant (or other source of water) and to a fire station; whether your community has a professional or volunteer fire service; and any other factors that can affect the time it would take to put out a fire.
- The condition of the plumbing, heating, and electrical system.

The price you pay for your homeowner's insurance can vary by hundreds of dollars, depending on the above data and the company. So shop around and get at least three price quotes. You can call companies directly or access information on the Internet. Your state insurance department may also provide comparisons of prices charged by major insurers.

SHOPPING TIPS FOR GETTING THE BEST INSURANCE DEAL

- *Get quotes from different types of insurance companies.* Some sell through their own agencies with the same name as the insurance company; others sell through independent agents, who offer policies from several insurance companies; and some don't use agents. You can even find insurers who sell directly to consumers over the phone or through the Internet.

• *Consider going with a higher deductible.* The deductible is the amount of money you have to pay toward a loss before your insurance kicks in. The higher your deductible, the more money you save on your premium. A deductible of $500 or $1,000 may save you as much as 25 percent.

• *Add the necessary riders.* If you live in a disaster-prone area, don't forget to factor in the cost of additional riders you'll need to cover your specific threat. For instance, if you live near the East Coast, you may need a separate windstorm deductible. In other areas you may need a separate deductible for hail storms or tornados. Sometimes when the cost of riders is added in, a policy is not as competitive as it looks at first.

• *Buy your home and auto policies from the same insurer.* Most companies that sell homeowner's insurance also sell auto and umbrella liability insurance. (An umbrella liability policy will give you extra liability coverage.) Some insurance companies will reduce your premium by 5 to 15 percent if you buy two or more insurance policies from them. But make certain this combined price is lower than buying coverage from different companies.

• *Make your home more disaster resistant.* Find out from your insurance agent or company representative what you can do to make your home more resistant to windstorms and other natural disasters. You may be able to save on premiums by adding storm shutters and shatter-proof glass, reinforcing your roof, or buying stronger roofing materials. Older homes can be retrofitted to make them better able to withstand earthquakes. In addition, consider modernizing your heating, plumbing, and electrical systems to reduce the risk of fire and water damage.

• *Insure the house, not the land.* You'll need to subtract the value of the land when you calculate how much homeowner insurance to go with. Too many homeowners insure their home for the appraised value that includes the land as well as the improvements. Insurance agents should point this out, but many times they don't because it increases your premiums and their profits.

• *Check out discounts for home-security devices.* You can usually get discounts of at least 5 percent for smoke detectors, burglar alarms, or deadbolt locks. Some companies may cut your premiums by as much as 15 percent or 20 percent if you install a sprinkler system and a fire or burglar alarm that rings at a monitoring station. These systems aren't cheap, and not every system qualifies for a discount. Before you buy one do the math. Find out what kind your insurer recommends, how much the device would cost, and how much you'd save on premiums.

- *Ask what other discounts are available.* Companies don't all offer the same type or amount of discounts in all states. Ask your agent or company representative about discounts available to you. For example, if you're at least 55 years old and retired, you may qualify for a discount of up to 10 percent. Or if you've completely modernized your plumbing or electrical system recently, you may get a price break.

- *Check out group coverage.* Check whether a homeowner's policy is available through your employer, and is a better deal. Also, professional, alumni, and business groups may offer insurance packages at a reduced price.

- *Ask about loyalty discounts.* If you've been insured with the same company for several years, you may receive a discount for being a long-term policyholder. Some insurers will reduce premiums by 5 percent if you stay with them for more than three years, and by 10 percent if you're a policyholder for six years or more. Still, rates and policies can and do change, so compare every couple of years to make sure you're getting the best deal possible.

- *Review policy limits and the value of your possessions annually.* You want your policy to cover any major purchases or additions to your home. But you don't want to spend money for coverage you don't need. If your five-year-old fur coat is no longer worth the $5,000 you paid for it, you'll want to reduce or cancel your floater (extra insurance for items whose full value is not covered by standard homeowner's policies).

Earthquake Insurance

Standard homeowner's, renters, and business insurance policies do not cover damage from earthquakes. However, coverage is available with an endorsement or as a separate policy through most companies. Unlike flood insurance, earthquake coverage is available from private insurance companies—except in California, where homeowners can also get coverage from the California Earthquake Authority (CEA).

The deductible for earthquake insurance is most often 2 percent to 20 percent of the replacement value of the structure rather than a set amount. Fox example, if it takes $100,000 to rebuild a home with a 2 percent deductible, you would be responsible for the first $2,000. Insurers in states like Washington, Nevada, and Utah, with higher than average risk of earthquakes, can have minimum deductibles of around 10 percent.

EARTHQUAKE INSURANCE INFORMATION

www.insurance.wa.gov/factsheets/factsheet_detail.asp?FctShtRcdNum = 20
www.answers.com/topic/earthquake-insurance

www.money.cnn.com/2006/10/16/pf/saving/toptips/index.htm?postversion =
    2006101615

Premiums differ widely by location, insurer, and the type of structure. Generally, older buildings cost more to insure than new ones. Wood-frame structures have lower rates than brick buildings because they tend to withstand quake stresses better. The cost of earthquake insurance is calculated on per-$1,000 basis. For instance, a frame house in the Pacific Northwest might cost between $1 to $3 per $1,000, while on the East Coast it may cost less than fifty cents per $1,000.

Flood Insurance, Who Needs It?

Homeowner's policies don't cover flooding. You can only get flood insurance from the federal government's National Flood Insurance Program (NFIP). It boils down to this: If you don't have an NFIP policy, you don't have flood coverage.

Even though you may live outside Special Flood Hazard Area (SFHA) boundaries—also called one-in-100-years flood elevation—the low cost of a NFIP policy may still be worthwhile.

Storm drains may overflow and flood adjacent areas, canals may break, and new developments may channel water where it's never gone before: your basement.

In fact, 25 percent of the 595,000 claims the Federal Insurance Administration has paid out since 1978 have been to people outside the flood zones.

FLOOD INSURANCE WEBSITES

www.fema.gov/nfip
www.floodsmart.gov/floodsmart/pages/index.jsp
www.info.insure.com/flood-insurance/who-needs-flood-insurance.htm
www.pueblo.gsa.gov/cic_text/housing/natlflood/insurance.htm
www.ambest.com/guide/flood.html

To find out if your home is in a flood zone, contact your local building or planning department and ask to see the flood insurance rate map published by the Federal Emergency Management Association, or FEMA. If your zone designation begins with an A or V, you're in a flood plain, and to obtain an

FHA, VA, or conventional financing you'll need proof of flood insurance prior to closing. Also, coverage is not limited to homeowners; tenants can purchase their own flood insurance policies covering contents.

Flood insurance can be purchased in any community that has agreed to adopt flood plain management programs. Currently, about 18,000 of the nation's 22,000 cities, towns, and counties are members.

Average premiums in high risk areas are about $300 a year. The rate goes up according to the value of the property and its location. But premiums in low and moderate risk areas are as low as $85 a year. Coverage tops out at $250,000, with an additional $100,000 for contents. The policies also covers up to $500 for removing contents to a safe location, and up to $750 for sandbagging, pumping, and other preventive costs.

Flood insurance policies are sold through local insurance agents. The company that handles your homeowner's policy can probably add this coverage for you.

MORTGAGE AND TITLE INSURANCE

Mortgage life insurance, title insurance, and private mortgage insurance (PMI) are the three types of insurance policies you're likely to need if you bought your home with less than 20 percent down.

Mortgage Life Insurance

Many people confuse mortgage life insurance with private mortgage insurance (PMI). Private mortgage insurance, discussed below, pays the mortgage lender in case of default. If you take out a mortgage with less than 20 percent down payment, the lender will require PMI to protect them from default. Although it sounds similar, mortgage insurance that insures you in case of disability or death is optional.

Within a few days of closing, you'll probably get offers and brochures from your mortgage company or an affiliate offering different types of mortgage life insurance. Some policies will make the payments if the borrower becomes disabled, others will pay off the mortgage upon death. The question is, are these policies a good way to go.

MORE INFORMATION ON MORTGAGE LIFE INSURANCE
www.money.cnn.com/2003/12/19/pf/expert/ask_expert/index.htm?postversion
= 2003121909

www.lifeinsure.com/lifeinsurance/mortgage.asp
www.insweb.com/learningcenter/articles/life-mortgage.htm
www.wtnh.com/Global/story.asp?S = 3599578

If you would sleep better at night knowing that if you became sick or disabled your mortgage payment would be paid, then this type of policy may be worth pursuing. Compare quotes from several insurers including the company that has your homeowner's policy. Rates will vary widely depending on area, age, and amount.

Another option available is the policy that pays off the mortgage if you die. Basically this is called decreasing term insurance. In theory, the rates should go down as you pay off the mortgage.

Many financial experts say a standard term policy is not only cheaper but has more flexibility. For example, mortgage insurance would pay off the mortgage balance automatically if you die. A regular term policy would pay the survivors, but if they don't want to pay off the mortgage they don't have to. Here again, the best way is to check with several companies and compare rates. The company that has your homeowner's policy may have this program and give you a cost break.

Title Insurance 101

In many states the purpose of the title company is threefold: 1) To sell title insurance, 2) to handle escrow funds, and 3) to handle the actual closing, where you go in and sign the paperwork. Other states have attorneys or escrow companies that do the actual closing. But regardless of who does the closing, title companies still provide the title insurance coverage on your property.

MORE INFORMATION ON TITLE INSURANCE

www.firstam.com
www.mtgprofessor.com/title_insurance.htm
www.homebuying.about.com/od/homeshopping/qt/TitleInsurance.htm
www.money.cnn.com/2006/01/11/real_estate/title_insurance_exposed/index
    .htm?cnn = yes

Title insurance is one of the biggest yet least understood costs in buying a home. It's one of those fees that you don't get involved in directly. And, like homeowner's insurance, it can have a big impact when the need suddenly complicates your life.

Charles and Kristen found this out when they thought they had bought a home on a half acre along a river. What the seller didn't tell them was that a few months earlier the county had bought an easement along the river for a parkway. This reduced the back property line by 40 feet and somehow the title search had missed the easement.

When Charles and Kristen were landscaping their backyard, a county parks employee came by to stake out the jogging trail. He told them they were encroaching on the future parkway. Understandably, the new homeowners were upset and called the title company. Luckily, their insurance was with a good company and they ended up with a fair settlement.

Typically, you (or the seller) pay a one-time fee at closing to insure the property against the following problems:

- Forgery and impersonation
- Lack of competency, capacity, or legal authority of a party
- Deed not joined in by a necessary party (co-owner, heir, spouse, corporate officer, or business partner)
- Undisclosed (but recorded) prior mortgage or lien
- Undisclosed (but recorded) easement or use restriction
- Erroneous or inadequate legal descriptions
- Lack of a right of access
- Deed not properly recorded
- Claims for adverse possession or prescriptive easement
- Deed to land with buildings encroaching on land of another
- Incorrect survey
- Silent (off-record) liens (such as mechanics' or estate tax liens)
- Pre-existing violations of subdivision laws, zoning ordinances, or CC&Rs (covenants, conditions, & restrictions)
- Post-policy forgery
- Forced removal of improvements due to lack of building permit
- Post-policy construction of improvements by a neighbor onto insured land
- Location and dimensions of insured land

As you can see, these are some heavy-duty problems that can ruin your day if they pop up unexpectedly.

In another sticky situation, Jack and Carolyn bought an older home in a small town. The tax notice described the property dimensions as 110 feet by

140 feet, which had been the accepted dimensions for seventy-five years and six buyers.

The new buyers decided to put up a fence, but when they measured 110 feet from the east corner they found their lot went about 7 feet into their neighbor's living room. This was a potentially messy situation.

Jack and Carolyn contacted the title company that insured their sale and they had a surveyor check out the property corners. As it turned out, the old town survey had a few problems. All the lot lines along the street had to be readjusted on the plat, and new property descriptions worked up and recorded in the county recorders office. It turned into a several-thousand-dollars project, which was covered by the title insurance.

Title insurance costs vary from state to state. Some states set the rates, others require that insurers file their rates with their state department of insurance, and some don't regulate the fees.

In Iowa, home buyers typically purchase a title-warranty certificate from the Iowa Finance Authority. You get the same coverage as title insurance at a fraction of the cost. Ask your Realtor or mortgage lender about the norm in your state.

Private Mortgage Insurance

Private mortgage insurance (PMI) is the third type of insurance policy you're likely to have if you bought your home with less than 20 percent down. Private mortgage insurers are usually separate companies that specialize in insuring mortgages. They're not connected to a government agency, mortgage company, or investors.

PMI insures the lender against you failing to make your payments and they having to foreclose. The monthly premium is calculated on a sliding scale. With a 5-percent down payment the premium will be higher than with a 10-percent down payment, and it is calculated as a percentage of the loan amount.

For instance, a $250,000 home with a 5-percent down payment might have a .70 percent premium. or $138.54 per month. A 10-percent down payment could have a .50 percent premium, or $93.75 per month. Your monthly rate can also depend on your credit rating as well as the loan amount.

Normally PMI is supposed to drop off when the loan is paid down 20 percent, but until recently many homeowners had been taking advantage of lower interest rates and rising house values to refinance and get rid of PMI. On FHA-insured loans, however, the PMI doesn't drop off. So a good strategy is get into the house with an FHA loan and then refinance to a conventional 80-20 loan as soon as possible.

THE SEVEN BIGGEST INSURANCE MISTAKES MANY HOMEOWNERS MAKE

1.   Not keeping careful and complete records of improvements, possessions, and other items in case your home is destroyed or damaged.

2.   Failing to review and upgrade your homeowner's policy yearly. Home values are going up so fast in some areas that if you had a disaster would your policy cover it?

3.   Not keeping a duplicate set of records and photos offsite so your data won't be destroyed if there's a problem.

4.   If you have an older home, not having a plan to upgrade those items that are not up to code. In case of a fire, for example, a homeowner's policy typically pays to rebuild to "as was" condition. Before you can get a certificate of occupancy, all systems will have to be up to current codes. It can be a case of "pay me now or pay me later."

5.   Failing to consider other threats in your area and the need for additional policies. If there's a problem, will you be stuck with a big mortgage and a damaged home without coverage?

6.   Not shopping around for the best rates or taking advantage of discounts offered by some insurers when you have your homeowner's and other policies with the same company.

7.   Failing to do a risk audit of your home and yard. This is where you look at your property and make a list of possible problems you need to correct. For example, let's say an old tree in the front yard is diseased and weakened. If an ice storm hits, will it end up crashing through your roof?

Some things you would look for when doing a risk audit are:

- Look at the trees around your home can that could fall and damage your home. You might want to hire an arborist to check them out if they're old or appear to have problems.
- Prune trees and branches that are too close to power lines or your roof.

- Are there areas around your home that could funnel water into your yard in case of a 500-year storm, a breached canal, or an overflowing creek or river?
- Are there a lot trees and bushes close to your home that pose a fire hazard? Would it be better to clear-cut everything away from the home to create a fire zone?
- Look at your home and yard with a "what if" mindset and note how you can make your home safer should the worst happen.

CHAPTER 10

AVOIDING THE TEN MOST COSTLY
HOUSE PROBLEMS

In this chapter you'll learn:

- ✓ The ten most common problems that homeowners encounter while buying or living in a home
- ✓ Suggestions on how to correct these problems
- ✓ Tips on preparing your home for sale

If you were to poll home inspectors, appraisers, Realtors, and remodelers on what problems they encounter most frequently, chances are their lists would be similar. The same problems appear so consistently that it's not too difficult to pick out the top ten.

Some of these problems are so common that many homeowners have learned to live with them; they no longer consciously register, not even the dangerous ones that can kill you.

You may want to check your home against the ten problems outlined in this chapter and see if you need to do some preventive maintenance. It's much cheaper to fix problems before they're flagged by an inspector or appraiser. Also, getting into a time crunch to get things fixed before closing usually costs you a lot more bucks.

For example, one home seller, who was a little on the lazy side, let maintenance slide for a few years. When he decided to put the home up for sale, it languished on the market for weeks until a handy couple made a low offer.

Unhappy with the offer but running out of time, the seller accepted it. However, when the home inspection report came back, it listed some wiring and roof problems the buyers insisted be fixed before closing. The seller had no choice but do the repairs if he wanted to keep the sale from falling apart. In the end, the seller sold the home for $12,000 under market and had to spend $3,700 in electrical and roof repairs. He walked away from closing with $15,700 less than he should have had.

Fortunately, these ugly equity-reducing situations don't have to happen, and you can avoid them by checking out the following ten most common house problems and their solutions.

PROBLEM ONE: FAULTY WIRING

Many electrical problems are caused by homeowners who try to cut corners by not using a licensed electrician or by trying to do the work themselves. This is one area where mistakes can have consequences you don't want.

One homeowner, for example, got a nasty jolt when she walked across a wet, freshly mopped floor and touched an ungrounded electric stove. The metal clamp that attached the grounding wire to a metal pipe had rusted through, creating an ungrounded system.

Luckily she wasn't badly injured, but she was one unhappy homeowner when she called an electrician soon after.

Common electrical mistakes to look for are:

- Open junction, switch, or receptacle boxes. Without faceplates, wires are exposed to kid's exploring fingers. Accumulations of dirt and lint can also cause a short. Face plates that were removed when a room is painted or remodeled need to be replaced promptly. Also, look in basements, attics, garages, or out-of-the-way places for electrical boxes that don't have faceplates.
- Dangling hot wires are especially dangerous. Homeowners sometimes remove light fixtures or reroute wires and forget to wire-nut the hot

wires. Always test any dangling wires to make sure they're not hot. Remove unused dead wires and label hot wires (safely wire-nutted in a box) so you know what breaker they're attached to.

> You can download an excellent electrical safety manual free in PDF format from: www.cdc.gov/niosh/pdfs/02-123.pdf.

- Especially if you have an older home, check and make sure the service cable, breaker panel, and main disconnect have the same amp rating. Owners sometimes try to upgrade wiring themselves and fail to match up all the system components. If you have an older system that's rated for less than 100 amps, you may want to consider upgrading to 150 or 200 amps.
- Make sure the grounding wire/clamp is attached to a metal pipe or stake. This is usually located next to the electrical service entrance. In older homes these clamps sometimes rust off, leaving the home ungrounded. That can shock you if you touch a metal pipe or appliance. Replace the clamp if it's rusty or not making good contact.
- If your home was built between 1964 and 1974 and you haven't upgraded your electrical, you should check for aluminum wiring. You can tell aluminum wiring by its dull gray color where it connects to the neutral bus bar in the breaker box. Unlike copper wiring, aluminum shrinks and swells, loosening splices and connections. A fire hazard can result if a wire becomes loose and shorts. As a result, aluminum wiring requires a special crimp connector (called a COPALUM connector) to connect to switches and outlets. Have a professional electrician inspect your wiring to make sure you have these types of connectors. (Oh, and keep the paperwork to show buyers the wiring is sound when you sell.)

> For more information on aluminum wiring go to: www.inspect-ny.com/aluminum.htm.

PROBLEM TWO: GRADING AND DRAINAGE PROBLEMS

Appraisers and inspectors often zero in on landscaping conditions that can allow water to drain toward the house or into a basement or crawl space.

Damage caused by this condition can not only lessen the value of the home but be very costly, since the restoration costs won't be covered by homeowner's insurance. You have to have government flood insurance to cover damage caused by an exterior water source.

Water damage from these conditions is often caused by:

- A home built on a hillside with poor grading funneling water to the foundation or low spots near the home.
- Poor drainage allowing landscaping bark or loose spongy soil to retain water, which will leak into the basement or crawl space.
- A valley location allowing water to concentrate near the foundation and leak into the basement.
- Careless backfill when the home is built, allowing water to easily penetrate the soil around the foundation.
- Soil settling or eroding around the foundation and allowing water to penetrate rather than run off.
- Downspouts and gutters not properly diverting water away from the foundation.
- Window wells not rising above grade.

Cures are to regrade the ground around the foundation for about 10 feet and slope it at least 4 inches. If the surrounding terrain is higher than the home, you can divert water by excavating swales and incorporating them into your landscaping.

INTERESTING WEBSITES ON GRADING

www.landscaping.about.com/od/sitegradingdrainage
www.taunton.com/finehomebuilding/pages/bh0028.asp

Also make sure gutters are functioning and cleaned out. You may need to add extensions to your downspouts to divert water away from the foundation.

Basement windows should be protected by wells that rise at least four inches above grade. On older homes, galvanized metal wells often rust through and need to be dug out and replaced. Water can also leak through basement windows when downspouts are carelessly placed too near a window well, or when sprinkler heads are not adjusted.

During the first good rainstorm after you move in (or before, if possible), grab an umbrella walk and around the house, looking for possible drainage problems. It's important to be proactive in this area, because water leaking into the house from an outside source is not covered by your homeowner's insurance policy.

PROBLEM THREE: FAULTY GUTTERS AND DOWNSPOUTS

When rain gutters, downspouts, and extensions work as designed, they do a great job keeping water away from the foundation and out of basements and crawl spaces. But if problems arise because components are missing or aren't installed correctly, it can be expensive to repair the water damage.

One homeowner failed to notice that a downspout strap had come loose, which allowed the leader to channel water into a basement window well. A heavy rainstorm put over a foot of water in the homeowner's finished basement.

Incidentally, because the water came from outside the home, the insurance company refused to pay for the damage. The homeowner ended up paying nearly $10,000 to replace carpets, sheetrock, and furniture, and to cover redecorating costs.

Clearly, constant vigilance is needed to make sure your gutters are and stay in good condition.

Some common gutter and downspout problems to check for are:

- Damaged sections that need repair or replacing
- Leaves and debris blocking water from flowing to the downspout
- Gutters too small to handle the runoff volume given the size of your roof
- No extensions on the downspouts to carry water away from the foundation
- Improperly installed gutters that fail to drain

RAIN-GUTTER WEBSITES
www.hometips.com/csprotected/guides/gutters.html
www.rainhandler.com/checkout.htm
www.home-ideas.org/Rain-Gutter-Installation.htm

To keep your gutter system working properly, clean out them out in the fall, and make sure water flows toward the downspouts. Seal small holes with silicone and larger ones with flashing and roofing cement.

If your home needs new or replacement gutters, check out contractors in the yellow pages. As with any other improvement project, get three bids before you commit.

PROBLEM FOUR: WATER IN THE CELLAR

A high percentage of homes either currently have or will have basement or crawl space water problems. Some have problems consistently, others only at certain times of the year because of seasonal conditions.

Whatever the source, you'll want to solve water problems as soon as possible to minimize damage and eliminate a potential deal killer when you sell your home.

Common water infiltration clues to look for are:

- Dark stains on floor or walls
- Water marks, or a pale powdery residue called *efflorescence,* on the walls
- Musty or unpleasant odors
- Mildew
- Recurring wet spots

Cures can be simple, or complex and expensive, depending on the problem. But before you panic and call a contractor, check out these possible solutions:

- Make sure the gutters, downspouts, and extensions are routing water away from the foundation.
- If the crawl space has a dirt floor, you may need to cover it with a plastic vapor barrier to keep water from migrating into the house.
- For small amounts of moisture migrating through walls, get water-proofing coatings that can be applied on the inside with a brush or roller. These are available at home centers and mail order.
- For bigger amounts of infiltrating water, you may need to install a *sump pump*. These are small pumps mounted at the bottom of a sump or shallow well. The pump has a float switch that kicks on the motor when water accumulates in the well. Since heavy storms are more likely to cause a power failure—which is when you need the pump working—you may want to consider adding a battery backup.

- Digging a trench around the foundation 18 to 24 inches deep, lining the bottom with crushed stone and burying a perforated pipe (curtain drain) can be effective.
- Cold water pipes, ducts, and water tanks can sweat a considerable amount of water. Insulating these moisture sources can reduce the problem considerably.
- Check for mold and keep it under control with bleach or other fungicide.
- If you have a floor drain, shine a light down it and make sure you can see water. If not, add water until you can. This is a vapor lock that keeps sewer gases out of your basement. Over time, the water can evaporate and allow unpleasant odors to escape.
- Never vent dryers into a basement or install a shower unless it has a fan that vents to the outside.

MORE DATA ON MOLD

www.traskresearch.com/mold.htm
www.epa.gov/mold/moldguide.html
www.cdc.gov/mold

PROBLEM FIVE: PROBLEM ROOFS

Few homeowners give their roof much attention until they discover a leak. Unfortunately, by then the damage is often extensive and expensive, as one owner found out when the kitchen ceiling crashed down onto the table. They had ignored a spreading stain in the ceiling, and it didn't take long until the wet sheetrock gave way.

Asphalt shingles, the dominant roofing material, have an average life span of 15 to 30 years depending on climate, exposure, and shingle quality. Because roof longevity can vary significantly even between homes that were roofed at the same time, it's critical to inspect your roof every few months.

Binoculars are good way to check the roof; there's no need to climb up and risk damaging shingles or falling off.

If you're thinking of selling your house and the roof is more than five years old, it's a good idea to get a professional roof inspection before putting it on the market. You don't want an inspector or appraiser finding problems after you've found a buyer. That can kill a sale or put you in a defensive position when a buyer threatens to walk unless you reroof.

Some common warning signs that your roof needs attention are:

- Asphalt shingles are curling and/or brittle and the valleys look worn. This means the roof is nearing replacement time.
- Flashings around vents, skylights, chimneys, and pipes are cracked and worn.
- Stepped flashing (flashing that is interwoven with the shingles) around the chimneys is curling and worn.
- Rubber collars that seal pipes at the roof line are cracked or worn. If roofing cement has been used to seal these joints, check for cracks or peeling.

MORE INFORMATION ON ROOFING

www.roofhelp.com/roof_repairs.htm
www.hometips.com/content/builtup_tp.html
www.hgtv.com/hgtv/rm

If you find problems in your roof inspection, some solutions are:

- New shingles can be applied over existing ones to cut costs. However, you should only do this once. More than two layers create excessive weight, especially in snow areas.
- A roof is only as good as its flashings. Make sure seals are replaced or recoated as soon they start to show problems. You may have to do this every year or two, depending on climate. Spending $50 or less to recoat is much cheaper than spending big bucks fixing water damage.
- If the roof looks like it may need replacing, get three bids from reputable contractors and compare.
- Don't go with 30-year shingles when you plan on living in the home only a few years. A buyer is unlikely to pay more for a 30-year roof than for a 20-year one.
- If you want to change roofing types—such as changing from asphalt shingle to metal, tile, or other type—check other homes around the neighborhood first. Spending thousands of dollars upgrading to tile when no one else has means you're unlikely to get your investment back when you sell.

PROBLEM SIX: FOUNDATION FLAWS

Older homes and even some newer ones can settle unevenly. Clues to uneven settling are:

- Obvious cracks in the foundation walls
- Cracks above door jambs and windows
- Sloping floors and ceilings
- Sticking or hard-to-open doors and windows

If a house has stabilized (you'll want a structural engineer to verify this), the cracks can be filled with hydraulic cement or similar caulking compounds that expand and seal. But if the problem is more serious, it could entail:

- Excavating the foundation and sealing cracks from the exterior side.
- If cracks go all the way through the foundation, sealing the inside as well.
- Replacing part or all of an unsound foundation. This can get expensive because the house would need be jacked up, the new foundation poured, and the home re-leveled. Obviously, this is going to be expensive, but the problem will have to be corrected before you can live in the home safely or sell it.

FOUNDATION INFORMATION WEBSITES

www.askthebuilder.com
www.inspect-ny.com/structure/foundation.htm
www.concretenetwork.com

One homebuyer did not hire a professional inspector because he worked in the building trades and felt he knew as much as any inspector. After the closing he was moving stuff into the basement, and when he moved some cardboard that was leaning against the wall he discovered a large crack. Water had started to leak through and discolored the concrete around the crack and down the wall. An inspector would certainly have caught this problem because this what they're trained to do.

Lesson learned: Even highly competent contractors can benefit from a professional inspection when they buy a home.

PROBLEM SEVEN: DEFERRED MAINTENANCE

If the home or yard isn't in good condition, it's not only a safety issue but a selling problem as well. Poorly maintained homes attract bargain hunters or investors who make steeply discounted offers. Homes that are in good condition attract top dollar and full price offers.

Keeping your home in top condition is not a cost, but an investment that will return more than you spend. To spread the costs out, some homeowners find fixing up and updating as they go along easier than having to max out a credit card when it's time to sell.

It's also much cheaper to catch problems up front before they get away from you and demand expensive solutions when you least expect it. This happened to one homeowner who had let maintenance items slide for several years. When health problems required him to sell the house, he couldn't do the necessary fix-up himself, and he didn't have the money to hire a professional to do it. As a result, the home sold for many thousands of dollars less than it should have. It was a good deal for an investor, but a bad deal for the homeowner who sorely needed all the money he could get from the sale.

Important maintenance items you'll want stay on top of are:

•   Paint rooms, ceilings, and trim as needed to keep your home looking good and send a message that you're serious about maintaining its quality.

•   Replace carpet or vinyl floors coverings when worn or out-of-date, This ranks second in maintaining a home's value. But if wood or tile floors are popular in your area, consider going that route for an up-to-date look.

•   Keep the caulking in showers and around tubs and fixtures watertight and in good condition. This will save you money by not having to replace a shower or tub enclosure because of water damage.

•   If a toilet starts leaking around the bottom, fix immediately. Damage from water seeping under the floor is a costly repair job.

•   Replace or fix leaking faucets. They not only waste water, but can stain sinks as well.

•   Keep the home's exterior in good condition. Caulk, paint, or fix sheathing problems immediately so insects and water don't invade and cause damage.

•   Keep hedges, bushes, and trees trimmed. One homeowner let his trees and bushes grow out of control for a few years. When he decided to sell he had to pay an arborist $1,700 to cut and prune the overgrown tangle.

• Seal and maintain driveways so water doesn't penetrate. When it freezes, it will destroy the surface and/or widen the cracks.

PROBLEM EIGHT: FAULTY PLUMBING

Water damage tops the list of homeowner frustrations and cost. But it doesn't have to be that way. It's important to remember that the water supply system is under pressure, and that water under pressure does interesting things, such as leave deposits in pipes and fixtures, corrode fixtures, and leak wherever there's a weak spot in the system.

Vigilance is the key to taming the water supply system. Keep a regular eye on the following:

• Water lines and fittings. Check the system every few months for leaks and hard water buildup on faucets and toilet components.

• If you have an older home and the pressure diminishes markedly as a toilet fills, the fixture or bathroom may be tied into a too small supply line. You may have to reroute the line to a better source. Old galvanized pipes could also have mineral buildup that constricts the water flow.

• If your water comes from a private well, you may need to check the pressure tank and pump. Sometimes a bigger tank can compensate for a low flow well.

• Replacing corroding pipes with newer lines is a good investment. New flex tubing makes replacing old water lines easier and cheaper than upgrading with copper.

• Trace any leak to its source immediately. Ongoing leaks ruin floors, wall studs, sheetrock, and other components that gobble up cash flow fast.

• If you're in a cold winter state, make sure pipes exposed to cold air are wrapped in insulation and/or heat tape. Check the heat tape connection daily. One duplex owner who shall remain nameless failed to do this and a pipe froze. By mid-afternoon when the pipe thawed, it split and water flooded the interior. The result was a costly restoration and unhappy tenants.

HELPFUL HOME-PLUMBING WEBSITES

www.plumbing-today.com
www.homeandfamilynetwork.com
www.hometips.com

The other half of a home's water system consists of the drain-waste-vent (DWV) pipes. Problems with this system show up when water drains slowly from a sink, tub, or shower. Causes can be:

1. Hair, food, or other material blocking the drain; it's an easy fix.
2. Mineral build-up in the drain pipes is a little more serious. Replacing the pipes with ABS pipes is the best long-term solution.
3. A vent pipe on the roof may be blocked, creating a vacuum that slows draining water. You'll need to get on the roof and make sure there's no obstructions in the pipe.

One serious indicator of a leak is water stains on a ceiling. A leaky shower pan, toilet seal, pipe or fixture has caused or is causing problems. For homebuyers this should be a red flag that signals potential water problems: Proceed with caution.

On the flip side, if you're a homeseller, and the water damage is evident, do what's necessary to fix the leak and restore floor, ceiling, or sheetrock to prior condition, pronto.

Once buyers see water damage—even though it's been fixed—they become skeptical, and your chances of a good offer go down the drain.

PROBLEM NINE: POOR VENTILATION

Although ventilation is one of those out-of-sight/out-of-mind home components, its effects on the house and your health are huge. For example, a poorly vented attic can heat up to 150 degrees in the summer, making it more expensive to cool. In the winter, water vapor condenses on insulation, rafters, and roof sheathing, causing rot and mold.

MORE VENTILATION INFORMATION
www.oikos.com/esb/39/VentOpt.html
www.askthebuilder.com/Ventilation.shtml
www.epa.gov/iaq/homes/hip-ventilation.html

Ventilation is an area that inspectors and appraisers will look at closely, and you don't want to have to deal with costly mold, roof rot, or adding vents a week before closing.

To prevent this:

- Keep gable vents open and free of nests, leaves, and debris.
- Inspect your attic every fall and spring for potential problems.
- If you finish your attic or add insulation, make sure you don't block soffit vents.
- Many older homes don't have enough attic ventilation, so you may need to install roof vents, wind turbines, or powered vents to keep outside air circulating. It's important to keep heat build-up in the attic to less than 15 percent of the outside temperature.
- A big no-no is venting bath, kitchen, dryer, or laundry fans into the attic (or basement). Fans should vent to the outside to prevent damaging water build-up.

PROBLEM TEN: DEFECTIVE HEATING SYSTEMS

As the Realtor walked through the home on a pre-listing inspection, he noticed the furnace was about twenty years old, and installed when the home was built. Knowing this was going to be an issue with buyers and inspectors, the agent suggested that the sellers get a furnace inspection ASAP.

A couple of days later the sellers called their agent all upset. The furnace contractor found the combustion chamber had cracked and that deadly carbon monoxide could escape into the home. This odorless and lethal gas could have easily caused serious problems for the homeowners. In fact, hundreds of people die from carbon monoxide poisoning every year in the United States.

In this case, the sellers replaced the furnace, the home sold a week later and the inspector found only a few minor problems. Lesson learned here is to have your furnace inspected yearly when it's more than five years old. Also important is when the sellers replaced their furnace, the new model was smaller, quieter, more efficient, and used less natural gas. Had they not sold their home, their fuel savings would have paid for the new furnace in less than seven years.

MORE INFORMATION ON FURNACES

www.aceee.org/consumerguide/topfurn.htm
www.energystar.gov/index.cfm?c = furnaces.pr_furnaces
www.furnacecompare.com/buying_a_furnace.html

Typically, inspectors and appraisers check gas or oil forced-air furnaces for cracks in the heat exchanger or combustion chamber. In a steam system, they look for cracks in the water jacket. If they find any, it usually means the furnace or boiler needs replacing.

Where the flue from gas water heaters and furnaces connect to the chimney is also a critical area, which should be checked every few months. A failure in the seal can leak toxic gas into the home.

Inspectors also check water heaters for bottom leaks—an indication of a rusted tank—and whether the pressure release valve is in good shape.

What are some things you can do to prolong your heating system?

•   Consider an annual service contract that ensures your furnace or boiler is properly cleaned and adjusted for the winter season.

•   Check chimney and flue junctions and make sure they are sealed and leak-free.

•   Replace the anode in the water heater. This is a device that attracts corrosion and prolongs the water heater tank life.

If you're thinking of selling your home, or if you have just bought a home and aren't sure about the condition of the furnace or water heater, contact an HVAC (heating, ventilation, air-conditioning) contractor for an inspection. Make sure they leave a sticker or tag on the furnace showing the date it was inspected.

Finally, if you have a forced-air furnace, it's a good idea to have the ducts professionally cleaned. It's amazing what collects around the vents and in the ductwork that you probably don't want to know about.

All ten problems discussed in this chapter are summarized in Table 10-1.

Table 10-1. Quick checklist for avoiding the ten most costly house problems.

Problem	Suggested Action
Faulty Wiring	Use a licensed electrician for upgrades and additions. Upgrade an older fuse box or 60-amp system ASAP. Look for uncovered boxes, dangling hot wires, and a poorly grounded system.
Grading and Drainage Problems	Make sure water drains away from the house, not towards it. Add extensions to downspouts to route water away from foundation and window wells. If needed, add clay or dense soil to create a slope away from the foundation. Perforated pipe buried in a ditch filled with crushed stone a few feet out from the foundation can help drain water.

Gutters and Downspouts	Clean and repair damaged gutters and downspouts. Seal holes. Make sure water isn't pooling around the foundation.
Cellar Moisture	Check drains for water in trap to prevent bad odors. Condensation problems from cold air may require heating the basement. Basement showers and dryers should be vented to the outside. Consider installing a sump pump for bad water leaks.
Leaking roofs	Reshingle, but not more than two layers. Check flashing around chimneys and valleys. Replace worn rubber collars that seal pipes and vents where they come through the roof.
Foundation Problems	Look for cracks in foundation walls, above doors and windows. Also look for sloping floors and sticking doors. Cracks and settling should be fixed by professionals ASAP before further damage occurs.
Poor Maintenance	Not keeping a home in good condition can lower its value thousands of dollars more than the cost of upkeep. To maintain its value, keep it painted, caulked, and keep the yard in good condition. It's also cheaper to correct problems as they occur rather than maxing out a credit card to do it all at once.
Faulty Plumbing	Check for low water pressure. Turn on a faucet and flush a toilet; if pressure falls significantly it may mean the supply line is inadequate. Look for leaks, especially around toilet and under sinks. Repair promptly or costly damage will follow. Keep drains clean and free of blockages. Check shower pan and tub caulking for leaks.
Inadequate Ventilation	Make sure attic has good ventilation. A rule-of-thumb is 1 square foot of vents for every 150 square foot of attic floor. If needed, install power vents or wind turbines. Vent bath, kitchen, and laundry fans outside and not into the attic or basement.
Furnace Problems	Shop around for an annual service contract, especially on furnaces older than five years. Check the water heater for corroded anode and replace if needed. Make sure chimney-flue connections are sealed and don't leak.

DEALING WITH DISASTER

Why do bad things happen to good homeowners? We don't know why, but when they do happen we can't call the super or landlord to bail us out; we must handle it on our own.

Although there are thousands of things that can go wrong, the following five are common problems millions of homeowners encounter every year. Also included are some suggestions to help you get started thinking about how to keep bad things from happening.

BAD THING #1: DEALING WITH A FIRE

You're on your way home from a late afternoon shopping trip when you round the corner of your street and see the flashing red lights of emergency vehicles in front of your home. Fire hoses snake from a hydrant down the street and two heavy-jacketed and helmeted figures are spraying water on a back corner of your house.

After fighting down a wave of panic, you run toward the house, trying to control the fear that everything inside is destroyed. Fortunately, you were lucky this time. One of the helmeted figures sees you standing there and walks over as he unbuckles his chin strap. He tells you the fire started in the laundry and only destroyed that room, the adjoining bath and some of the family room.

Once the firefighters have left, you'll have to decide quickly how much of the cleanup you're willing to do yourself. If the damage is extensive, leave everything as is and call your insurance agent immediately so the damage can be documented.

However, if the damage is light and limited to one room, you likely can start cleaning up on your own after calling your insurance agent. Some ways to clean up smoke damage are:

• Start out with a wet/dry shop vacuum to clean up soot and chemical foam from extinguishers. Open windows and door to circulate air through the home. Carpets, clothing, and furniture will require professional cleaning to remove the smoke damage.

• Although the insurance company will refer you to companies that specialize in these kinds of cleanup, it's likely they won't be able to get started for a few days. If you can get a head start and make the home livable, you'll minimize the disruption to your life.

• Dry cleaning sponges work well for removing soot particles from latex paint surfaces. Start on the ceilings and work down. When the sponge surface becomes saturated, simply scrape it off. For oil-based paints, vinyl wallpaper, and greasy kitchen fires, use a sponge and a grease-dissolving cleaner or detergent.

• If the home is unlivable, you'll need to board up broken windows and other holes. Remove as many valuables as you can and consider hiring a security service to keep an eye on the home.

> Check out The Institute of Inspection, Cleaning, and Restoration Certification (IICRC) at www.certifiedcleaners.org, or 800-835-4624, for a list of professionals who handle interior damage in your area. For info on how to file an insurance claim go to: www.iii.org/individuals/homei/help/howclaim.

BAD THING #2: HANDLING A WATER LEAK

Have you or someone you know ever come home from a vacation, or even after being away just a few hours, to find water running out the front door or a basement rapidly filling up?

Water problems can come from failed washer supply hoses, pipe joints leaking, splitting water lines, or even from someone forgetting to shut off a faucet.

Obviously, the first step is to try and turn off the water to the leaking line or fixture. If that proves difficult, you'll need to shut off the main water valve. Some suggestions are:

• In cold areas, you'll likely find the house shutoff valve in the basement, on the wall facing the street or where the supply pipe enters. If you have a private well, either shut off the valve on the supply line coming out of the pressure tank, or shut off the power to the pump.

• In warmer areas, the valve could be outside. If you can't close or find the valve, call the city water department immediately.

• Make sure the water hasn't come in contact with any outlets or cords before you go wading in, it could be carrying an electrical current. Shut off the main breaker, but if you can't get to it, call the power company and wait for them to cut the power.

• If the water damage is extensive, call your insurance agent. You may also need to call a cleanup company that handles water damage.

• If you have access to power, use a wet/dry vacuum, but make sure the circuit is connected to one with a ground-fault interrupter.

• For flooded basements, you'll need to rent a sump pump or gas powered unit that mounts outside and uses intake and discharge hoses.

• If the water is sewage contaminated, it's best to have a professional company disinfect the flooded area. Sheetrock and flooring may have to be replaced. Everything that got wet has to be thoroughly dried out to prevent mold.

• Don't throw away anything (soaked carpet, damaged furniture, etc.) until the insurance adjuster has had a chance to document your loss.

BAD THING #3: HANDLING A ROBBERY

The panic of finding your door ajar when you return home can blind you to the reality that you could be in danger. The thief/thieves could still be in the home. Before you enter, call 911 on your cell phone or go to a neighbor's home and wait for the police. Some tips to handle a robbery are:

• Don't go in or touch anything until the police arrive and process the home for fingerprints or other evidence.

• Be prepared to give the police a list of items missing and any receipts you may have. You'll also need this information for the insurance claim.

• Once the police find the point of entry, you need to repair any damage and beef up security where the burglars entered.

• Go through your home and do a security check; making sure you have deadbolts that meet ANSI Grade 2 standards on all entry doors. Also, check sash locks on windows to make sure they're secure. Clear out trees branches and bushes that can give thieves cover.

• If you haven't already done so, make up a list of valuables along with photos or video clips.

> For some downloads on home security, check out this website: www.ncpc.org/publications/brochures/protecting.php.

BAD THING #4: DEALING WITH A POWER OUTAGE

Fortunately, most outages don't last too long.and may only interrupt your computer. But in case of a blizzard or ice storm, a blackout is likely to last a long time. If that happens, here are some suggestions:

• Turn off any electrical devices you were using and pull plugs on electronic equipment. Disconnecting the main breaker can help keep surges from damaging anything when the power come back on.

• Fill containers with water. If the blackout is widespread, water pressure may soon drop. On a private well, keep the water in the pressure tank for drinking only. You may also want to fill bathtubs and containers for flushing toilets and nondrinking water uses.

• Never use a gas oven, kerosene heater, or outdoor cooker for heat unless you have good ventilation, like a partially opened window. Keep in mind that any flame heat source produces carbon monoxide, which can kill you fast.

• If the weather is below freezing, keeping water pipes from freezing is a major concern. When no other heat source is available, open faucets enough to allow a pencil thin stream of water to run. This should prevent pipes from freezing.

• Food will stay cold for up to three days, even during the summer, as long as you keep the refrigerator and freezer doors closed.

• Don't run generators in the garage or an enclosed area. Also, before kicking on the generator, shut off the main breaker so you don't send power into the main lines.

• Most important, put together a power outage kit of several five gallon containers of water, propane or Coleman camping type stoves, two or three propane lanterns, flashlights, extra food, and a couple of propane heaters.

BAD THING #5: DEALING WITH A DOWNED TREE THAT HIT YOUR HOUSE

When a heavy windstorm topples a tree onto your house, resist the urge to climb up on your roof, especially if it's steeply pitched. This is a job for pros with the right equipment. Otherwise:

• Inspect the underside of the roof from the attic. If the plywood decking or rafters are damaged, you're going to need a roofer. Your first concern is keeping water out of your home and preventing further damage.

• If the roof isn't damaged and is still water tight, then it's a matter of carefully cutting up and removing the limbs with pruning shears and bow saws.

• Chain saws should not be used on a ladder or on roofs where the footing is unstable.

• You'll likely find some damaged shingles. To patch these areas, use a piece of aluminum flashing to cover and slip under the shingles. You may have to remove some nails so the patch will fit. Apply asphalt roofing cement to the edges of the patch where you've inserted it under the shingles. This should hold it in place and keep out water.

• You can also use heavy plastic sheeting for a temporary patch, but you'll need to secure it by nailing furring strips around the edges. Sometimes a bead of roofing cement around the edges of the sheeting will hold it in place, unless you're expecting high winds and rain.

• It a good idea to assemble a roof-patching kit to have on hand. When disaster strikes you may not be able to get to a hardware store. Your kit should have several tubes of roofing cement, heavy 8–12 mil plastic sheeting, a couple of squares of aluminum sheeting, 20 to 30 feet of furring strips, roofing nails, claw hammer, and hacksaw.

AVERAGE LIFE EXPECTANCY OF YOUR HOME'S COMPONENTS

In the United States, few components wear out before they end up in the trash or at a demolition yard (see Table B-1). Features, styles, and efficiency of use change constantly, and homeowners upgrade every few years to keep up. Your home's components seldom have chance to wear out.

However, one great reason to upgrade is to replace a less energy-efficient appliance or building component with a one that is considerably more efficient. For example, if you have a refrigerator that is fifteen years old or older, you would probably save energy and money by replacing it with a new unit that uses 30 percent less power. The same can be said of water heaters, windows, doors, insulation, and flooring.

So, if you have a component that is approaching the end of its average life span, you should consider replacing it without feeling too guilty. You can save serious money if you keep your eye on sales and closeouts for the best deals, rather than waiting until an appliance fails.

Table B-1. How long you can expect your home's components to last.

Item	Average life
Dishwasher	10–12 years
Refrigerator	12–16 years
Clothes dryer	10–14 years
Microwave oven	8–10 years
Electric range	15–20 years
Gas range	18–20 years
Cast iron tub	50 years
Fiberglas tub/shower	10–15 years
Toilet	50 years
Laminate countertop	10–15 years
Ceramic tile countertop	50 years +
Wood countertop	15–20 years, if cared for
Granite countertop	20 years +
Interior hollow-core door	20–25 years
Interior solid-core door	30 + years
Exterior door, protected	60 + years
Exterior door, unprotected	20 + years (exposed to weather)
Garage door	30 + years
Garage door opener	10 years
Wood floors: oak or pine	50 + years (depending on care)
Slate flooring	50 + years
Vinyl flooring	10–20 years (less if you have a dog)
Central air conditioner	15 years
Electric water heater	12–15 years
Gas water heater	10–14 years (less for hard water)
Gas furnace	15–20 years
Heat exchanger	20–25 years
Wood deck	15 years, if you use a water protectant
Brick or concrete patio	24 + years, if sealed and no frost damage
Asphalt driveway	10 + years, if resealed every few years

Wood fence	12+ years, if recoated every few years
Asphalt shingle roof	15–30 years, depending on shingle quality
Wood shingles	15+ years, depending on climate
Tile roofing	50+ years
Slate roofing	50–100 years
Sheet metal roofing	25+ years
Wood siding	10 to 100 years, if it's recoated every few years and there is no water damage
Metal siding	50+ years
Aluminum siding	20–50 years
Vinyl siding	50 years

ENERGY SAVINGS AND A GREENER HOME

An important part of improving your home's interior is making it as energy efficient and green as possible. Table C-1 lists what you can do around the house to make that happen without spending big bucks.

Table C-1. Checklist for energy savings and a greener home.

Action	What to Do
Buy energy efficient appliances.	Check out www.energystar.gov for a list of energy-efficient appliances and home improvement information.
Replace single pane with double pane widows.	Shop for windows that are ENERGY STAR-rated. You may be eligible for a federal tax deduction of 10 percent of the purchase price.
Insulate pipes.	Insulate attic, ductwork, pipes, and water heater
Lower water usage.	Replace shower heads with low flow (1.5 gallons per minute or better) heads. Replace older toilets with newer, low-use models. Replace leaking faucets promptly.
Install bathroom fan (to reduce mold and mildew).	Fan should move 50 to 100 cubic feet of air per minute to the outside. Vent should be at least 4 inches in diameter to be effective. Also consider putting a timer on the fan.
Vent kitchen.	ENERGY STAR fans use up to 65 percent less energy and are quieter as well.
Clean your home.	Vegetable-based, environmentally friendly cleaning products and homemade cleaners can get the job done without causing skin and respiratory problems. Check the labels at grocery stores for these kinds of products.
Reduce power consumption.	Use compact fluorescent bulbs instead of incandescent bulbs, which use 50 percent more power.
Prevent heating and cooling losses.	Make sure doors and windows are sealed. Check outlet boxes, bedroom closets, and attic insulation.
Keep your furnace working efficiently.	Replace the furnace filter once an month.
Adjust your thermostat.	Make your home 1° to 2° cooler and you won't notice the change except when the utility bill arrives.
Decorate with indoor plants.	With today's airtight homes, indoor air quality can be improved with plants. Check with a local nursery for plants that work best in your area.

INDEX

Look for These Exciting Real Estate Titles at
www.amacombooks.org/gorealestate

A Survival Guide for Buying a Home by Sid Davis $17.95

A Survival Guide for Selling a Home by Sid Davis $15.00

Are You Dumb Enough to Be Rich? by G. William Barnett II $18.95

Everything You Need to Know Before Buying a Co-op, Condo, or Townhouse by Ken Roth $18.95

Make Millions Selling Real Estate by Jim Remley $18.95

Mortgages 101 by David Reed $16.95

Mortgage Confidential by David Reed $16.95

Real Estate Investing Made Simple by M. Anthony Carr $17.95

Real Estate Presentations That Make Millions by Jim Remley $18.95

The Complete Guide to Investing in Foreclosures by Steve Berges $17.95

The Consultative Real Estate Agent by Kelle Sparta $17.95

The Home Buyer's Question and Answer Book by Bridget McCrea $16.95

The Landlord's Financial Tool Kit by Michael C. Thomsett $18.95

The Property Management Tool Kit by Mike Beirne $19.95

The Real Estate Agent's Business Planner by Bridget McCrea $19.95

The Real Estate Agent's Field Guide by Bridget McCrea $19.95

The Real Estate Investor's Pocket Calculator by Michael C. Thomsett $17.95

The Successful Landlord by Ken Roth $19.95

Who Says You Can't Buy a Home! by David Reed $17.95

Your Successful Career as a Mortgage Broker by David Reed $18.95

Your Successful Real Estate Career, Fifth Edition, by Kenneth W. Edwards $18.95
